HONORING THE BODY

Meditations on a Christian Practice

Stephanie Paulsell

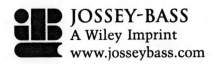
JOSSEY-BASS
A Wiley Imprint
www.josseybass.com

FIRST PAPERBACK EDITION PUBLISHED IN 2003

Published by Jossey-Bass
A Wiley Imprint
989 Market Street, San Francisco, CA 94103-1741   www.josseybass.com

Jossey-Bass books and products are available through most bookstores. To contact Jossey-
Bass directly call our Customer Care Department within the U.S. at (800) 956-7739,
outside the U.S. at (317) 572-3986 or fax (317) 572-4002.

Jossey-Bass also publishes its books in a variety of electronic formats. Some content that
appears in print may not be available in electronic books.

Credits are on p. 199.

Library of Congress Cataloging-in-Publication Data

Paulsell, Stephanie, date.
      Honoring the body: meditations on a Christian practice
/ Stephanie Paulsell.
         p.   cm.—(The practices of faith series)
         Includes bibliographical references and index.
         ISBN 0–7879–4856-X (alk. paper)
         ISBN 0-7879-6757-2 (pbk.)
         1. Body, Human—Religious aspects—Christianity. I. Title.
II. Series.
BT741.2 .P38 202
233.5—dc21   2001004959

FIRST EDITION
HB Printing   10 9 8 7 6 5 4 3 2
PB Printing   10 9 8 7 6 5 4 3 2 1

The Practices of Faith Series
Dorothy C. Bass, Series Editor

———

Practicing Our Faith:
A Way of Life for a Searching People
Dorothy C. Bass

Receiving the Day:
Christian Practices for Opening the Gift of Time
Dorothy C. Bass

Honoring the Body: Meditations on a Christian Practice
Stephanie Paulsell

Contents

———

Foreword

———

I
n this time of rapid social change and widespread spiritual seeking, many people yearn for a way of life that is good in a deep sense and attuned to the presence of God. Yet the contours of such a way can be difficult to see. What might it mean to live with integrity and hope when the pace of existence is accelerating and life's patterns are in flux? What is the shape of a life lived in right relation to other people, to the created world, and to God? Is it possible to imagine not just getting by but flourishing—as individuals, as communities, and as a global society, in concert with creation and in communion with God?

Such questions are in the hearts and minds of many seekers who are exploring spirituality today. Whether they grew up beyond religious communities or left the religious households of their childhood, they are now searching for some context of larger belonging and some pattern of believing and valuing that is richer and deeper than that offered by the wider culture. And life-long Christians are pondering these questions as well, longing for a profound and relevant understanding of what Christian faith has to do with their work, with friendship and marriage, with the way they raise their children, with public life and politics, and with how they use their time and money.

The Practices of Faith Series offers help drawn from the deep wells of Christian history, belief, and experience to people who long for a way of life that can be lived with integrity in our time. Books in this series focus on the *practices* through which Christian people seek to live in response to the love and grace of God. Practices are shared activities that address fundamental human needs; when woven together over time, they form a way of life. Reflecting on Christian practices, seekers and those who belong to other traditions will discover insights into matters of human flourishing that are of urgent concern to all thoughtful people, while Christian readers will encounter fresh perspectives on their long-cherished beliefs.

In *Honoring the Body,* Stephanie Paulsell invites readers to explore a practice without which we quite literally cannot live, but which is nonetheless severely endangered. At the core of this practice is that most fundamental fact about ourselves and others—embodiment, and with it the capacity for pleasure and suffering, for exertion and rest, for generativity and death. And yet today the human body—so intricate and capable, and yet so vulnerable—is threatened by dishonor, as a few impossibly "perfect" bodies are glorified while many, many others are despised as the wrong weight or the wrong color or the wrong something else. Paulsell does not recoil from directing our gaze to the terrible treatment some bodies receive, but her guiding purpose is to disclose how a Christian practice can guide us into a better way. Other aspects of the same practice encourage honor for the body in its strength and pleasure. Paulsell explores the moves and gestures of this practice—the washing of feet, the sharing of food, a baby's bath, and many more—within the context of everyday life, while also surrounding contemporary practice with a cloud of biblical and historical witnesses. All of these are in turn surrounded by God's embrace of the human body, which is created in God's own image, known by God in the incarnation of Jesus, and made newly alive, though still bearing wounds, in Jesus' Resurrection.

Stephanie Paulsell's hope for those who read this book is that you will find here resources for developing a sustainable practice of honoring the body within the uniqueness of your own daily life. My hope for the readers of all the books in this series is the same. I urge you to find companions with whom to discuss, pray about, and live each Christian practice, perhaps with the help of the *Guide for Conversation, Learning, and Growth* that accompanies each book and is free online at www.practicingourfaith.org.

Valparaiso, Indiana   Dorothy C. Bass
November 2001   Editor, Practices of Faith Series

For Kevin and Amanda

Preface

———

The poet Jane Kenyon once wrote of "the long struggle to be at home in the body, this difficult friendship." Who of us does not have intimate knowledge of just how difficult a friendship this can be? If you have ever worried over your body's size and shape, you know what Kenyon means. If you have ever been frustrated by the limitations of your body, you know the struggle she speaks of. If you have ever experienced your body more as a source of shame and confusion than as a source of delight, you know how hard it can be to feel at home in the body. A difficult friendship indeed.

And if you have ever wondered how to celebrate the body's pleasures and protect the body's vulnerabilities in a world that seems confused about both, you know how much we need practices that honor the body. We have, it seems, plenty of information about how to deal with certain anxieties about the body. Scientists direct us to certain foods that can protect our bodies from disease, magazines tell us how to lose weight or have better sex, health clubs and gyms promise "the body you've always wanted." But somehow these suggestions for our individual bodies fail to satisfy in any deep and lasting way.

In this book I'd like to offer another way of entering into the difficult friendship with our bodies, a way born of the conviction that embodiment is a sacred gift. I want to suggest that we have the resources for a rich practice of honoring the body in the accumulated wisdom of religious traditions. As a Christian, I know that my own tradition has long struggled with unease about the body. But I also know that sustained attention to the vulnerabilities and the sufferings, the pleasures and the confusions of the body has helped faithful people throughout history to deepen their relationship with God and others. Can such attention also help us fashion a practice of honoring the body from the accumulated wisdom of past and present? I believe it can. It will not be just an individual practice, however; it will be a shared, communal practice, one we engage in with others.

In the first two chapters, I will explore resources from Christian faith for a practice of honoring the body and discuss a set of unavoidable tensions about the body that will help shape the practice. I will then invite you to explore with me how we might honor the body in activities that punctuate our daily lives: bathing, clothing, eating, working, exercising, loving, and suffering. We will seek wisdom from scripture, history, and contemporary experience, in story and song and poetry.

My hope is that by reflecting on our bodies in everyday life we might cultivate a mindfulness about our own bodies and a more attentive consciousness about the bodies of others. I'll tell you the stories I have to tell about bodies bathing, dressing, eating, striving, loving, suffering. I hope that, in return, you'll meditate on your own stories and grow into a deeper sense of the mystery and sacredness of your body and others' bodies. I hope you will find resources here to construct a sustainable practice of honoring the body in the uniqueness of your own daily life.

This book is born of the desire for a way of life that cherishes the body. It is a book about how to honor the body at its limits of birth and death, but perhaps more important, how to honor the body during the days and years in between. It is a book for parents who long for the well-being of their children. It is a book for the girl whose long sleeves hide the marks of self-mutilation, or who throws up her meals in secret. It is a book for the boy who wonders if steroids might help him build the sculpted body he wishes he had. It is for all those who wish fervently for a different body and those whose lives are governed by the work of keeping the body a certain size and shape. It is for those whose bodies have been violated. It is for anyone who finds in athletic exertion a way to connect with the world and others, and it is for those who still cringe at the memory of grammar school recess. It is for the lover who delights in the body of the beloved. It is for those living with debilitating illness and those who love and care for them. It is for those who know the bodily longing for God that the psalmist describes in Psalm 63 when he writes, "My flesh faints for you as in a dry and weary land where there is no water" (Psalm 63:1).

This book is for anyone who wants to know how to honor her or his own body and the bodies of others and for anyone who wants to teach others to do so. It is for those who wish for a community that cherishes bodies, attends to their needs, celebrates their pleasures, and soothes them in distress. It is for those longing to honor the body in gestures large and small, in ordinary life and in extraordinary circumstances, in every moment of every day.

Cambridge, Massachusetts　　　　　　　　Stephanie Paulsell
November 2001

Acknowledgments

———

I n 1994, Dorothy C. Bass and Craig Dykstra invited
me to join their seminar on Christian practices.
They have been important teachers and mentors for
me ever since. I am grateful to them for their wisdom,
encouragement, and friendship—and their conviction
that honoring the body is an indispensable practice of the
Christian life. The remarkable members of the practices
seminar, who eventually became the authors of *Practicing Our Faith: A Way of Life for a Searching People* (1997),
have inspired me in my writing and in my living. Several
members of the seminar have accompanied me in the
writing of this book, especially Dorothy, Craig, and Greg
Jones, whose colleagueship and critical wisdom I could
not do without.

The Valparaiso Project on the Education and For-
mation of People in Faith, a project of Lilly Endowment
Inc., supported me in the writing of this book. I am

grateful to Susan Briehl, Christine Pohl, and Don Richter, colleagues through the Valparaiso Project, who read and responded to a great deal of this book and made important suggestions.

My editors at Jossey-Bass, Sarah Polster and Sheryl Fullerton, asked all the right questions and offered challenging intellectual companionship as I worked on this book. I am exceedingly grateful to them. During the writing of this book, Sarah died after a difficult illness. This is a terrible loss for me and many others. I hope I have written a book that would have pleased her.

I wrote this book while teaching at the University of Chicago Divinity School. It was my privilege to work for two outstanding deans, W. Clark Gilpin and Richard A. Rosengarten. I am grateful not only for their willingness to help me arrange more time for writing but also for reading my work and offering wise and constructive responses.

My students in the ministry program at Chicago influenced this book in many ways—through class discussions as well as through the example of their own practices of faith. Several students read portions of this work, some allowed me to read their own theological writing on the body, and some entrusted me with their stories of embodiment. I'd like to thank especially Hilary Copp, Chad Herring, Jennifer Kottler, Anna Lee, Loretta McGrath Miller, Elizabeth Marquardt, Elizabeth Musselman, Joy Omslaer, Angela Thinnes, Diana Ventura, and Amy Ziettlow.

Many of my colleagues at Chicago discussed the

ideas of this book with me and responded to my writing. I am particularly grateful to Alison Boden, Don Browning, Catherine Brekus, W. Clark Gilpin, Paul J. Griffiths, Margaret Mitchell, Richard A. Rosengarten, and Elena Vassallo. Kristine Culp and Kathryn Tanner's writings and friendship have been especially important to me, in particular Kristine's work on ecclesiology and on pilgrimage and Kathryn's work on Christian practices, notably in her book *Theories of Culture: A New Agenda for Theology* (1997).

My neighbors in Chicago, Patricia Evans and Jamie Kalven, helped me think about what it means to honor bodies that have experienced violence, through conversations in our shared backyard, through Jamie's book *Working with Available Light: A Family's World After Violence* (1999), and through the many ways they honor their bodies and the bodies of others in their everyday life.

Three writers whose work I admire—James Carroll, Serene Jones, and Parker J. Palmer—read this book in manuscript and offered support for which I am deeply grateful. I finished the book in Cambridge, Massachusetts, where Claudia Highbaugh, the chaplain of Harvard Divinity School, taught me how deeply body and soul can be nourished through meals shared with friends.

Portions of this book were presented at retreats and workshops. I'd like to thank especially Dean Kristine Culp and the Disciples Divinity House of the University of Chicago, the Public Theology Workshop at the University of Chicago Divinity School, the community of

Holden Village, the Christian Women's Fellowship of Kentucky, St. Mark's Episcopal Church of Evanston, Illinois, Ebenezer Lutheran Church of Chicago, and the 2001 Spirituality Conference at Montreat Conference Center. I am grateful for the rich conversations I experienced in these places.

Kay Bessler Northcutt embraced this project with her whole heart from the beginning, sharing with me her ideas about how we might honor our bodies, urging me to tell the truth about embodied life, and allowing me to tell some of her stories. My debt to her is immense. Amy M. Hollywood gave me the benefit of her deep knowledge of feminist theory and human thinking about the body as I worked on this book and made crucial suggestions on every chapter. René Steinke helped me think through several difficult issues and read with care everything I sent her. I am grateful to these three remarkable writers for their generous interest in this project and for their friendship, which has deepened my life in every way.

My parents, William and Sally Paulsell, have been teaching me how to honor the body since the day I was born, and they are teaching me still. My sister, Diane Paulsell, has given me the benefit of her profoundly moral perspective on the body. I am grateful to my parents and my sister for reading and commenting on each chapter, for allowing me to tell some of their stories, and for the compassion and wisdom with which they live their lives.

I thank my husband, Kevin Madigan, for sharing

with me his historical and theological knowledge and for reading the whole manuscript with his keen editorial eye, thereby saving me from some (although probably not all) of my worst instincts. I am grateful to my daughter, Amanda, for reminding me through the exuberance of her play of the pleasures of embodiment. Kevin and Amanda are in many important ways the impetus for this book. It is their bodies that greet me each day, their bodies in which I most delight, their bodies I wish so much to nourish and protect. And it is to them that I dedicate this book, with love, gratitude, and hope.

S. P.

HONORING THE BODY

Chapter 1

AWAKENING TO SACRED VULNERABILITY

———

My desire for a practice of honoring the body was awakened the day I crossed the threshold of the hospital to the world outside after the birth of my daughter.

For two nights, nurses had purposefully entered and exited my room, bathing my daughter, weighing her, swaddling her. While I clumsily tried to feed her at my breast, crying from the pain of it, unsure of how to hold her properly, the nurses amazed me by how expertly they fit her into the crook of their arms, how tightly yet comfortably they wrapped her in a blanket, with what sureness they bathed and dressed her. The whole universe of the hospital seemed to lean attentively toward her and every other baby on the floor, watching them carefully, monitoring their weight, keeping their small bodies clean and dry. Inside the hospital everything seemed geared toward protecting and caring for the most vulnerable of human beings.

When the time came to leave, a nurse carried my baby to the door that separated the hospital from the parking garage. There, she handed my daughter to me and bid me farewell and good luck. Even with my mother on one side of me and my husband on the other, I found the prospect of walking out of the hospital terrifying. My ability to feed and care for this tiny stranger seemed to me very much in doubt. My hands were not as practiced as those of the nurses, my touch not as sure.

I also knew, with sudden clarity, that I was bringing my daughter into a world more complicated than the maternity ward, a world that was not organized solely for the care of children's bodies. Outside, on a snowy, cold Chicago day, cars were zooming by, exhaust was being expelled, ice had formed on the sidewalks. So many dangers to a little body. We settled her in the infant car seat, and I leaned across her for extra protection. With the emergency blinkers flashing, my husband drove us through the icy streets toward home.

The world my daughter entered that day is infinitely more interesting than the hospital. In this world, she is a body, but she is also more than a body. In this world, there is more to honoring the body than keeping it clean and dry. In this world, my daughter will need not only to be bathed and fed but also to be embraced and respected, offered freedom and love. In this world, when the body is honored, the whole person is honored. And when the body is dishonored, the whole person is harmed.

The threshold between the hospital and the world outside is only one of many thresholds my daughter will cross that will illuminate the vulnerability of her body. She has ahead of her the thresholds of adolescence and adulthood, of sexual awakening, of birth, perhaps, and certainly of death. My dearest hope is that as she crosses these thresholds, she will know her body not only as vulnerable but as sacred.

What I desire with all my heart is to be able to invite her into a way of living that teaches her, through the countless bodily gestures of everyday life, to cherish and honor her body and the bodies of others. I want her bathing and her dressing, her eating and her drinking, to remind her that her body is a sacred gift and nurture within her a profound compassion for the vulnerabilities of all bodies. I want her to have such reverence for the body, and to know her own body as so deeply cherished, that she is able, if she wishes, to enter joyfully one day into a long and loving intimacy with another person, an intimacy in which she both receives and gives pleasure and deep, sustaining comfort.

You don't have to have given birth to a child to feel daunted by the task of caring for the body of another. Adoptive parents know what this feels like every bit as much as birth parents do. So do new teachers confronted by a roomful of preschoolers who want to climb everything in sight. So do those who attend to aging relatives. So does anyone who has ever cared for those whose lives have been interrupted by violence, accident, or serious illness.

Awakening to Sacred Vulnerability

And you certainly don't have to have given birth to a child to feel unsure of how to honor the body in a world in which some bodies are held up as perfect and desirable while others are despised. It's no wonder we are confused about how to honor the body when, all around us, bodies are used to sell products, and our anxieties about the appearance of our bodies are manipulated to sell even more. You don't have to have given birth to a child to desire a new way of life that honors our bodies, that chooses reverence over exploitation and anxiety.

FAITH AND THE WISDOM OF THE BODY

Where can we turn for help? Where can we go to learn the sacredness of the body? Where might we discover practices that can give shape to a way of life that honors the body? How can we resist the dishonoring of our bodies and intervene against the dishonoring of the bodies of others?

We can begin by looking to our neighbors. Every day, often without any grand theories to guide them, ordinary people honor their bodies and the bodies of those around them. The family that makes time to share a meal together, in the midst of everyone's busy schedule. The man who gives his beloved a daily bath, when his beloved is living with AIDS and can no longer bathe himself. The teacher who brings music to her classroom and invites her students to dance. The teenager who

gives up smoking. Women who gather in a church base-
ment to learn techniques of self-defense. Workers who
organize so that they can insist on regular breaks from
repetitive manual labor. Lovers who reverence each
other's nakedness. If we look, we will see all around us
people honoring the body in ways that are sometimes
simple, sometimes playful, sometimes heroic. But in all
of these gestures and activities, however spontaneous or
improvised, the sacredness of the body is encountered
and clarified.

To use the word *sacred,* of course, is to imply that we
can turn to religious traditions for wisdom about the
body. But what do religious traditions have to offer the
lover, the worker, the caregiver, the child? As a Christian, I believe that there is a long history of honoring the
body in Christian traditions, an accumulated wisdom
with which we might fashion a contemporary practice of
honoring the body. But I also have to acknowledge that
Christians have inherited an ambiguous legacy about the
body. Christianity has long struggled with an uneasiness
about the body, even as it affirms the goodness of the
body in its bedrock beliefs. Many people have experienced religious traditions not as repositories of wisdom
about how to honor the body but as repressive institutions
that deny the goodness of the body and its pleasures, or
as beliefs that nurture animosity toward particular bodies. If the man bathing his incapacitated beloved has seen
Christian demonstrators on the evening news shouting
"God hates queers" at the funeral of a gay man murdered
because of his sexual orientation, it is understandable that

he might not think Christianity has anything to offer him. If the newly married couple remember a childhood filled with sermons about the evils of sex, they might not think to turn to Christianity to find language for their gratitude for the delight their sexuality brings them.

Theologian Kathryn Tanner defines Christian practices as doorways through which we enter an argument. Through Christian practices, she says, we participate in an argument over how best to live as disciples of Christ and learn to live our way into new and unexpected answers. I wish, in this book, to join an argument about the body that has been going on for centuries. I wish to argue that it is possible to discover in scripture, history, and contemporary life the contours of a distinctively Christian practice of honoring the body that has wisdom to offer our culture. The practice of honoring the body reflects the ways Christians have responded to the needs that all human beings share—the need to be sheltered and nourished, protected and loved—in a way that bears witness to God. It is a practice not meant to be hidden within a Christian society separated from the wider world but to be shared with all God's people. Indeed, it is a practice shaped by all God's people.

But this practice is not just lying on the surface of scripture and history, like a stone in the road. It has to be excavated, argued for, and put into dialogue with all the ways that contemporary people do and do not honor the body. Tanner reminds us that Christian identity is an ongoing task that demands our creativity, our eagerness to place our faith and our lives in conversation, our willingness to be challenged and changed. The fashioning of life-giving practices from the wisdom of the past and the present is a sign of the creativity of the life of faith itself.

TOUCHSTONES FOR THE PRACTICE OF HONORING THE BODY

The convictions, wonderments, and hopes that orient Christians to God and the world form the bedrock upon which the Christian practice of honoring the body is built. As both Jews and Christians affirm, God judged creation good, and so everything God created, including bodies of all sorts, is good. The opening chapter of the book of Genesis bears witness to this, and to another conviction about the body—that God created human beings, male and female, in God's image. For Jews and Christians alike, the body reflects God's own goodness.

The affirmation that every body is made in the image of God is supplemented in Christianity by the belief that God was somehow fully present in a particular human body that lived in a particular time and place, the body of Jesus of Nazareth. The church has used the word *incarnation* to describe the conviction that God was *incarnate,* enfleshed in a body that ate and drank, slept and woke, touched and received touch. This body also suffered a death as painful and degrading as any human beings have devised. Early Christian testimony that this

Awakening to Sacred Vulnerability

body also lived again after death shapes a profound Christian hope that undergirds the practice of honoring the body. Whatever else it means, the Resurrection of Jesus suggests that bodies matter to God. And they ought to matter to us, too.

Convictions about creation, incarnation, and resurrection hold the body at the center of Christian life, where it influences how Christians worship and how Christians understand themselves. Christians regularly gather in worship for the Lord's Supper, a meal modeled on the last meal Jesus ever ate with his closest friends and followers. The Lord's Supper reminds us that every meal can be a time to draw closer to one another and to God. But this particular meal nourishes us with bread and wine, the same simple food that Jesus shared with his disciples during their last meal together, food of which he said, This is my body. This is my blood. It is Jesus' wounded body that gathers us for the Lord's Supper, Jesus' wounded body that makes inescapably visible all wounded bodies and nourishes compassion for them.

In worship, we sit, we stand, we kneel. We bow our heads, we stretch out our hands. In worship our bodies are taught to praise and to plead, to make and receive offerings of care and forgiveness. In the Lord's Supper, God offers us food and drink. In baptism, our bodies are washed clean. In the passing of the peace, we touch one another in love and hope. In worship, our bodies are disclosed as God's gracious gift.

Early Christians even thought of themselves, the fledgling church, as the body of Christ. Unlike many other religions of the day, Christianity was not an association solely of free men. A gathering of Christians was a gathering of diverse bodies, including women's bodies and enslaved bodies. All of these bodies were members of Christ's own body, the early church believed, and "members one of another" (Romans 12:5).

Just as the different members of a human body all have different functions, so do members of the body of Christ possess particular gifts that enable them to take on the work of Christ in particular ways—often in ways that disrupt society's expectations about how certain bodies ought to behave. By choosing the metaphor of the body to describe themselves, early Christians acknowledged that it is through our bodies that we love and serve God and one another. Although early Christians sometimes seemed to mistrust the body by opposing the body to the spirit, they did not call themselves the spirit of Christ. They called themselves the body of Christ, taking up the work of Christ's own hands and feet, head and heart, with their bodies—healing, preaching, caring for the outcast and the defenseless, suffering imprisonment and worse.

These, then, are the touchstones for a contemporary Christian practice of honoring the body. That God created our bodies good. That God dwelled fully in a vulnerable human body. That in death God gathers us up, body and all. That through our bodies we participate in God's activity in the world.

In one of his most challenging teachings, Jesus claimed that when we honor the bodies of others, we honor him. And when we dishonor the bodies of others, it is him we wound. Jesus taught that we encounter him in all who hunger or thirst, in the stranger and the prisoner, in those who are ill and those who are unclothed and unsheltered. So every time we offer food and drink to someone who is hungry and thirsty, or receive a stranger with kindness, or visit a prisoner, we tend to Christ himself. And every time we withhold our help, it is Christ we refuse (Matthew 25:31–46). This is the distinctive Christian contribution to a contemporary practice of honoring the body: the conviction that every body is worthy of blessing and care and that through the needs of the body, we are invited into relationship with God.

EMBODYING SPIRITUALITY

The practice of honoring the body is a vital aspect of Christian spirituality. But spirituality is often understood as being made up solely of what individuals do alone, like solitary prayer, meditation, and spiritual reading. And because what is "spiritual" is often opposed to what is "bodily," these activities are often understood as somehow disembodied, as if they engaged the mind and spirit alone.

In fact, disciplines like prayer and reading and meditation are deeply embodied activities that are indispensable to the cultivation of our life with God. But life with God is shaped both in silence and in conversation, in solitude and in community. The important thing is to be able to find paths that lead us back and forth between our prayer and our work, our meditation and our world. Our attention to God and one another can and must be shaped in communal ways as well as in solitary ways, through worship with others, through action on behalf of others, and in the ordinary stuff of our daily lives with others. Without practices that help us seek God's presence in the ordinary moments of our lives, we will miss countless opportunities to draw near to the God who made us.

Honoring the body is a practice that cuts across the boundaries between the individual and the community. The body marks our individuality, to be sure. Our bodies are separate from all other bodies in a profound way. In spite of what the book of Genesis says about lovers becoming "one flesh," we never truly become one flesh with another, no matter how intimate our relationship. We cannot fully know another's inner life. We can keep secrets from one another. But our bodies also make it inescapably clear that we cannot do without one another.

This is so because of the profound vulnerability of every human body, a vulnerability born, in part, from our separateness. We cannot feel pain in another's body, nor can others experience firsthand pain in our own. When we are in pain, we must rely on the ability of others to imagine that pain. And we must hope that imagination will lead to compassion.

Our bodies are vulnerable in other ways as well. If we have an abnormal pap smear, find a lump in our groin or breast, or feel pain when we urinate, we cannot ignore the vulnerability of our body, no matter how well we eat or how much we exercise. If we are worried about the appearance of our body—our weight, or the condition of our skin, then we know all too well the many ways we are rendered vulnerable by our body. If we desire the love and touch of another person, we are made vulnerable by our hope to be desired in return.

Our fragile bodies require communal attention, and so honoring the body is a shared practice, one for which we need each other in profound ways. Think of all the times you have needed someone to care for your body, or times when you offered care to another. It takes a village, as the saying goes, to raise a child. And certainly, children need caregivers who will touch them with love, shield them from harm, and feed them nourishing food. But young people encountering the pleasures and pains of sexual desire for the first time also need a village. They need guidance and support from communities that openly articulate sexuality as a good gift. People who are so sick that they feel their bodies have betrayed them need to be touched by those who believe deeply in the goodness of the body. When I was in labor, I needed my husband to press ice to my lips, to cradle me during contractions. I needed the midwife to hold my face in her two strong hands and say, "Oh *yes,* you can do this. Women have done this for *centuries.*"

Christian conviction about the goodness of the body, coupled with a recognition of the body's vulnerabilities, has nurtured a profound sense of responsibility for the protection and nourishment of bodies throughout the history of the church. The fourth-century Christian scholar Jerome taught that the body was the great equalizer of persons: "He whom we look down upon, whom we cannot bear to see, the very sight of whom causes us to vomit, is the same as we are, formed with us from the self-same clay, compacted of the same elements. Whatever he suffers, we also can suffer." Bodily vulnerability is something we all share—rich and poor, male and female, enslaved and free. Early Christians preached that knowledge of such shared vulnerability must lead us to solidarity with every other human body, especially the bodies of the poor. These Christians knew that what is suffered by one can be suffered by all, and that every body is a fragile temple of God's Spirit and worthy of care.

Chapter 2

PONDERING THE MYSTERY OF THE BODY

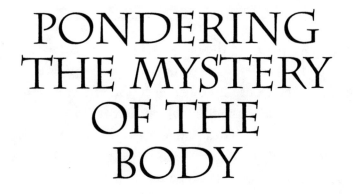

As we search for resources in scripture, history, and contemporary experience, we will find much that will answer our desire for a way of life that honors the body. But we can also expect to find a set of tensions about the body that illustrates our need for the practice: tensions between being a body and having a body, between integrity and relationality, between freedom and constraint, and between sacredness and vulnerability. It is essential that we meditate on these tensions. Not only do they remind us of how much we need a practice of honoring the body, they also caution us to guard against the ways this practice might be corrupted.

BEING A BODY AND HAVING A BODY

What is this body we wish to honor? There seem to be as many descriptions of the body as there are people to describe it. The body is a friend or a traitor. A gift or a task. Something precious knit together by God's own hands or the prison house of the soul, which, according to Plato, is trapped in the body like an oyster in a shell. Most descriptions of the body tend to fall into one of two camps: some suggest that the essence of who we are is merely encased, temporarily, in a body. In other words, a body is something we *have*. Others suggest that what is essential about human being cannot be separated from our bodies. In other words, we *are* our bodies in a very fundamental way.

Although these are two very distinct ways of understanding the body, the truth is, most of us do not seize once and for all on one description or the other, but rather move and back and forth between the two. When, during vigorous exercise, we find ourselves drawing on hidden reserves of energy and stamina, it is easy to feel that our body is an integral, irreplaceable part of our self. If we have been diagnosed with cancer, however, it is just as easy to feel that our body has become our enemy, that it is an inadequate container for the person we truly are. In the course of our daily lives, we probably operate with a double understanding. We can feel, in some moments, that our body is a deeply integrated part of ourselves. In other moments, we can feel deeply alienated from it. The fact that we can feel both ways—in the course of a single day, even perhaps in a single moment—points to the difficulty of defining just what the body is.

This tension exists in religious traditions as well. In the Hebrew Bible, the human person is never described as made up of separable parts like "body" and "soul." Rather, the whole human person *is* both soul and body. Being human means being both strong and fragile, full of both life and death. According to the Hebrew Scriptures, we *are* our bodies, just as we *are* our souls. One is not better than the other; both are irreplaceable parts of the human person.

In the New Testament, this wholistic understanding of the human person enters into conversation—and sometimes into conflict—with the classical Greek notion that the soul is the highest, finest aspect of human being. In the world in which Christianity took shape, the body was often regarded as the prison cell in which the soul is trapped, a temporary aspect of one's identity. But even though this vision of the human being was so powerful in the world from which Christianity emerged, Christian notions of incarnation and resurrection constantly called it into question. There were some early Christians who tried to argue that Christ's humanity must only have been an illusion, since something as precious as divinity could never dwell in a vulnerable human body. But that notion never gathered enough strength to persist in Christian communities. The basic Christian conviction that God had indeed been present in a human body endured, subverting all

Pondering the Mystery of the Body

attempts to deny the goodness of the body and its integral place in the human person.

The tension between being a body and having a body is perhaps most apparent in the writings of the early Christian teacher, Paul. Longing for the freedom God offers, he feels constrained from embracing that freedom by the unruly desires of his body. "For I delight in the law of God in my inmost self, but I see in my members another law at war with the law of my mind, making me captive to the law of sin that dwells in my members. Wretched man that I am! Who will rescue me from this body of death?" (Romans 7:22–24). This cry of the heart reflects the very human frustration over the way the body's frailties render us "captive." But Paul also believed that we draw near to God with our bodies. Indeed, he believed that the body is a holy place within which God might come to dwell: "Your body is a temple of the Holy Spirit within you," he wrote to the members of the church at Corinth. "Glorify God in your body."

Do we inhabit a body, or is a body who we truly are? Both views of the body have profound implications. If we believe that we *are* our bodies, we might give greater value to the human body than if we thought it was only the shell that our true self inhabited. But we might also place the fulfillment of our bodily desires above every other consideration, or we might allow ourselves to be defined wholly by our bodies. If we believe that we simply *have* a body, we might resist such constraining self-definition. But we might also come to view the body as somehow distinct from who we are. And we

HONORING THE BODY

might gradually come to see the body as a hindrance or, at the worst, something to despise.

I have been helped, in pondering what the body is, by the poetry of Mark Doty—especially his poems about the illness and death of his partner, Wally Roberts, from AIDS. It is when the body's vulnerability is most fully exposed, as it is in illness, that the question about what the body is becomes so acute. Doty's poem "Atlantis" is in part a meditation on this question. Here is the third section of that poem, entitled "Michael's Dream."

Michael writes to tell me his dream:
I was helping Randy out of bed,
supporting him on one side
with another friend on the other,

and as we stood him up, he stepped out
of the body I was holding and became
a shining body, brilliant light
held in the form I first knew him in.

This is what I imagine will happen,
the spirit's release. Michael,
when we support our friends,
one of us on either side, our arms

under the man or woman's arms,
what is it we're holding? Vessel,
shadow, hurrying light? All those years
I made love to a man without thinking

how little his body had to do with me;
now, diminished, he's never been so plainly
himself—remote and unguarded,
an otherness I can't know

the first thing about. I said,
You need to drink more water
or you're going to turn into
an old dry leaf. And he said,

Maybe I want to be an old leaf.
In the dream Randy's leaping into
the future, and still here; Michael's holding him
and releasing at once. Just as Steve's

holding Jerry, though he's already gone,
Marie holding John, gone, Maggie holding
her John, gone, Carlos and Darren
holding another Michael, gone,

and I'm holding Wally, who's going.
Where isn't the question,
though we think it is;
we don't even know where the living are,

in this raddled and unraveling "here."
What is the body? Rain on a window,
a clear movement over whose gaze?
Husk, leaf, little boat of paper

and wood to mark the speed of the stream?
Randy and Jerry, Michael and Wally
and John: lucky we don't have to know
what something is in order to hold it.

Such is the mystery of the body. Sometimes we
know that we are our bodies, that our capacity for life
and death makes us who we are. At other times, we feel
that we simply inhabit a vessel that is inadequate to con-
tain all that we are. But at all times, it is the body that allows us to reach out for one another, to steady each other

on our feet when we are weak, to embrace one another in joy and in despair. Thank God we don't have to know what something is in order to hold it.

INTEGRITY AND RELATIONALITY

Our bodies help us draw near to one another, but they also keep us separate from one another. Only when we are in our mother's womb are we truly one flesh with another, and that time is short. When, after hours of laboring and pushing, my daughter slipped out of my body into the world, my first thought was, *Who are you?* I had a sudden sense of her otherness, the uncountable ways in which she was not me. At the same time, when I saw her knees and elbows and tiny round heels, I recognized her; I knew what she had felt like pressing against the inside of me. Now that our bodies had taken up separate spaces in the world, a new moment in our relationship began. But this new relationship was mediated by our bodies every bit as much as was the relationship we developed when she was still living inside my womb. Just as we had begun to know each other through her flutters and kicks and turns, our knowledge of one another deepened as I slept curled around her, as she pressed her face against my breast, as I bathed her head to toe, memorizing her. I remember waking up one morning to the delicious smell of her nestled against me. Almost without thinking, I licked her forehead. So hungry to know her, I tasted her skin.

Pondering the Mystery of the Body

In such moments, it is easy to see that our bodies exist both in relation to other bodies and in the integrity of their own boundedness. Even in the most intimate of relationships, secrets can be kept, held in the body. Even in the most intimate of relationships, one can never know fully the inner life of another, nor can one share another's bodily experiences. We cannot respond to another's bodily needs and desires with compassion unless we have the capacity to imagine those needs and desires. But even though our bodies are distinct from the bodies of those closest to us, it is through our bodies that we are also able to enter into relationship with others.

Sometimes the tension between the integrity and the relationality of the body is made manifest in terrible ways. Jamie Kalven writes in his book *Working with Available Light: A Family's World After Violence* of his struggle to understand the pain and the irrevocable knowledge about the world that his wife, Patsy Evans, held in her body after being raped and badly beaten while out for a run one autumn afternoon. Patsy had come to know what those who have not endured such violence can perhaps only understand theoretically: that it is possible to be ripped out of the world in a second, unmoored from the web of relations from which we take our identity. That the same body that connects us with spouse and child can be reduced in a moment to the object of another's cruelties. "There is knowing, and there is *knowing*," Patsy said. Even a loving, intimate couple cannot share the knowledge each holds in her or his body without deliberate acts of attention, imagination, and compassion. Jamie's story is the story of a husband's strenuous attempt to share somehow in the terrible knowledge that his wife carries in her body.

Survivors of violence understand in a profound way the tension between the body's integrity and its relation to others. To be held in the grasp of a cruel, violent person is to know what it is to be isolated in your own body and yet to be bound to another, against your will, through your body. We occupy our bodies separately, but our bodies bring us into relation with others. Everything depends on how those relations are formed—with gentleness or cruelty, attention or disdain. Reaching out for the body of his wounded beloved, Jamie ponders with despair that "tenderness and cruelty can occupy the same space in the world. All it takes is two bodies."

For Patsy, the relationality of the body provided a point of resistance to the violence inflicted on her. In the midst of the attack, she caught a glimpse of a cyclist on the path where her assailant had grabbed her. "She looked like an angel," Patsy remembers. The sight of another human being broke into the unbearable isolation into which the rapist had forced her with the intensity of revelation: "When I saw the woman on the bike path, I thought, oh God, I'm not dead yet. The world is still out there." She broke away and ran toward the woman on the bicycle, toward another human being, toward all that connects us with the world and one another. Although Patsy resists any easy consolation, including narratives that identify her as courageous, I am in awe of her courage.

Pondering the Mystery of the Body

The integrity of the body is another point of resistance to violence and oppression. In our culture, some bodies are constructed to be more relational than others. Women socialized into being endlessly hospitable, endlessly welcoming, are one example. Although hospitality can be a powerful practice for the good, those whose bodily and psychic boundaries are too permeable can easily fall prey to those who would transgress that openness to inflict harm. If an abused spouse understands herself only as a body in relation, the integrity of her body is vulnerable to repeated trespass. If adolescents experiencing the first stirrings of desire can only see their bodies in relation to the bodies of others, they are vulnerable to coercion by those who would make selfish use of their bodies. Maintaining a strong sense of the body's integrity in the midst of the body's many relations is a crucial aspect of the practice of honoring the body.

Another important aspect of the practice is to recognize that our bodies bring us into relation not only with those nearby but also with those far off in ways we rarely acknowledge in the course of everyday life. The air conditioners we use to keep cool in the summer eat away at the ozone layer we all need to survive. The meat for some of the quick, convenient fast foods we consume comes from cattle raised on large stretches of land in impoverished countries which might have been used for local people to grow needed food. Choices we make about our individual bodies can have effects on the bodies of others we will never meet. Truly, we are members one of another.

Such is the wisdom of the Christian tradition on the integrity and relationality of our bodies. God made us separate from one another, but with the potential to be in relationship with one another. The integrity of our bodies is a gift from God, but the meaning of our bodies does not stop at the boundaries of our skin. For we belong to one another, and so we are called to attend to the effects of our choices. We belong to one another, and so we have a share in one another's joy and a responsibility to help one another bear grief and pain. The cultivation of the practice of honoring the body can help us remember that in both our integrity and our relations with other bodies, we belong to God.

FREEDOM AND CONSTRAINT

Jews and Christians have often sought freedom through practices that seem at first to constrain the body. The laws contained in the books of Exodus, Leviticus, Numbers, and Deuteronomy give instructions about what to eat and what not to eat, what to wear and what not to wear, when to bathe, when to work, when to rest. To an outsider, these laws may seem terribly constraining, an impediment to the freedom of the individual. To many practitioners, however, a life lived according to the law is a life ordered toward freedom.

As an example, we might take the commandment to keep the sabbath holy. The observance of the sabbath can seem a great constraint on freedom. Martin Luther, for example, famously wrote, "If anywhere the day is made holy for the mere day's sake, then I order you to work on it, to ride on it, to feast on it, to do anything to remove this reproach from Christian liberty." In our own culture, it seems at the least bad time management to refrain one day each week from work and commerce, and at the most a severe constraint on our freedom to make or spend more money. But the sabbath commandment is not a reflection of God's desire for the limitation of our lives; rather, it reflects God's care for us, God's intention that we all be free. As any faithful sabbath keeper can tell you, refraining from work and worry, making and spending, frees us to taste and see that God and the life God offers us are very, very good. The practice of sabbath keeping teaches us that the world can do without our work for one day and that God is the ultimate source of our work's energies. It also teaches us to desire and work for a world in which everyone has both enough work and enough time off. Dorothy Bass, a contemporary Christian sabbath keeper, reminds us that only free people can take a day off. The commandment to keep the sabbath holy is an enduring testimony against slavery and reflects the freedom that God desires for all people.

Christian practices involving the body often reflect the same tension. Practices that seem to constrain the body often have freedom as their motive. Early Christians, for example, looked for clues about humanity's relationship to God in the moments when the body seems stripped of freedom—in sexual desire and in death.

HONORING THE BODY

Some believed that death revealed our separation from God most fully. Many of these Christians understood sexuality as God's gracious gift, offered in sympathy for our mortality because it offered a remedy for it, through procreation. Others thought that sexuality itself was the clearest sign of our distance from God, because sexual desire can assert itself insistently even when the individual wills otherwise. The Christian practice of honoring the body took shape within the very human concern over how the basic physical realities of death and sexual desire can rob us of our freedom. At their best, early Christians aimed to restore human freedom in the face of those powerful forces.

Early Christians shocked their fellow citizens and the leaders of the Roman Empire when some chose sexual abstinence over family life. Marriage and procreation were highly valued by the Roman Empire, because families generated more citizens, more soldiers, more cities. The body was a commodity that ensured the empire's growth. When some early Christians abstained from marriage, they claimed that their bodies belonged not to the empire but to God. Later, as some Christians formed celibate communities dedicated to prayer, sexual abstinence also offered freedom, particularly to women. Rather than marrying at an early age, giving birth to many children, and perhaps dying young as a result, some Christian women found, through the sexual abstinence practiced in women's monasteries, the freedom to become educated, to be leaders, to write, and to preach and teach.

In our own day, it is not sexual abstinence but sexual fidelity that can seem to constrain human freedom. And, indeed, pledging oneself to remain faithful to one person for a lifetime is no small thing. It means saying no to other potential sexual relationships, even when other relationships seem to promise a heightened sense of excitement and joy. But it can also mean saying yes to sexual pleasure that deepens and intensifies over time and to intimacy spacious and elastic enough to hold the lifelong hopes and struggles of two people who are both united and kept separate by their bodies. The practice of honoring the body will not make questions of sexual expression less complicated but will help us hear in those questions a call for discernment in matters of freedom, pleasure, and love.

Fasting is another constraining practice that can offer freedom. As part of keeping the season of Lent, for example, Christians often fast from certain pleasures—chocolate, caffeine, and alcohol are favorite renunciations—in order to prepare an unencumbered space for receiving the good news of Easter. Like pregnant women who deny themselves small comforts—a cup of coffee, a glass of wine—in order to offer their developing child the most freedom possible in which to thrive, observers of Lenten renunciations give up certain bodily pleasures to sharpen their attention to the story of life and death that Lent and Easter embody. In a body newly attentive to its needs and hungers, the story of Lent and Easter has the freedom to unfurl as year after year the story yields new meanings.

Of course, any powerful practice, like sexual abstinence or sexual fidelity or fasting, can be used for good or ill, for freedom or for constraint. The same practice that allowed early Christians to claim the autonomy of bodies made in God's image was also used to deny the goodness of God's gift of sexuality. The same practice that allowed women freedom for learning and leadership was used to support a fear and even hatred of women and women's bodies. Fidelity is wielded like a weapon when it is used to keep someone in an abusive or deadening relationship. Renunciation of food and drink becomes destructive when it is used not to sharpen attention but to punish oneself. Because any powerful practice can be corrupted, we must be attentive, as we fashion a contemporary practice of honoring the body, to the ways in which our choices about our bodies can lead us toward the freedom that God intends for all of us, as well as how they might dishonor the body and cause harm.

SACREDNESS AND VULNERABILITY

In the Free Will Baptist churches of my home town, the quarterly communion service always includes the intimate work of foot washing. The whole church gathers in the sanctuary for prayers and the Lord's Supper, and then the community separates, women into one room, men into another.

Pondering the Mystery of the Body

When I was in high school, I sometimes attended these services with friends. I can't say for sure what went on in the men's gathering, but I imagine it was very similar to the ritual enacted among the women. After receiving communion, we would leave the sanctuary in twos and threes, trying, I will admit, to link up with a good friend whose feet we would wash and who would in turn wash ours. Once we had all gathered, the older women would begin singing "Amazing Grace." We would all join in, singing it over and over until everyone's feet had been washed.

Each pair of women was given a basin of water and a long towel, long enough to tie around your waist, long enough to gird yourself, as the Gospel of John says Jesus did when he knelt to wash the feet of his disciples. One woman would sit in a chair, take off her shoes, and place her feet in the basin. The other woman would kneel down in front of her, wash her feet in the water, and then dry them off with the ends of the towel. To me, the drying seemed more intimate than the washing. The washing was simply a matter of swirling water around the top of the foot that rested in the basin. To dry this foot, however, you had to take it in both your hands, prop it on your knee, and rub it, top and bottom, with the towel.

Unlike the Free Will Baptists, most churches have not made the washing of feet a sacrament to be enacted regularly within the community. The lesson of the act, exemplified by the story of Jesus washing the feet of his followers in the thirteenth chapter of John's Gospel, is emphasized instead. And certainly, it is not in ritually washing the nice clean feet of our best friends that we most truly follow Jesus, but in doing justice and seeking to live compassionately among all people.

But when we focus on the interpretation of the act without participating in the practice of it, we miss some important things. We miss, for instance, the startling, excessively intimate experience of handling the feet of another and putting our own feet in another's hands. Even those churches that do sacramentalize foot washing try to mitigate the intimacy of the act, as the church I visited did when it separated the women from the men—as, in fact, we all did, when we scrubbed our feet thoroughly before leaving for church.

But it is precisely the scrupulous toenail clipping and prechurch scrubbing of feet that points to the real gift of foot washing. For our attempts to have clean, sweet-smelling feet to offer betray the many ways we are rendered vulnerable by our bodies. When you offer your feet to another to be washed and gently dried, it is impossible not to notice the difficult relationship between our bodies and our identities. And when you kneel to wash the feet of another, you glimpse the vulnerabilities that attention to the body can evoke. I have only participated in foot washing three or four times in my life. But I can imagine that, practiced over a lifetime, this ritual might nourish a new vision of the relationship between the sacredness and the vulnerability of the body.

The kind of new vision I'm talking about is the kind that is granted to first-time parents, who fear they will break their baby the first time he or she is put into

Pondering the Mystery of the Body

their arms. It is the vision that is bestowed upon new parents who are unsure of how to hold a baby, much less change a diaper or offer a breast. It is the new vision that comes when you are the only thing keeping the tiny, floppy baby you are bathing from drowning in the bath water, and you suddenly know, really *know,* how vulnerable children are in our hands, how utterly dependent they are on those who care for them. So every time you soap your child's back, or scoop the shampoo off her forehead, or turn her body in the tub, it is impossible not to remember that some children are in the care of persons who are not gentle, but who are angry and violent. And so bath time becomes a time of prayer, prayer for all children, not just your own.

The kind of vision I mean is the terrible vision inflicted on the woman who has been raped of the long history of the violation of human bodies. It is the vision of the woman whose agonized compassion for those in every time and place who have endured such violence interrupts her sleep and her appetites. It is the vision of her grieving husband, gently massaging her wounded body, and seeing, as if for the first time, how fragile the human body is.

All of these moments of new vision, the joyful and the terrible, are glimpses into God's view of us. In Psalm 103 we find that God's compassion for us is born of God's knowledge of our frailty. God knows how we were made, the psalmist writes. God remembers we are dust. The father lowering his baby into the bathroom sink, taking care not to nudge the hot water valve, sees his child the way God sees us. The woman grieving the damage done to vulnerable human bodies sees others the way God sees us. The man urging a glass of water on his dying partner sees him the way God sees us.

And although she probably doesn't realize it, the teenage girl holding the foot of a friend in both her hands is being taught to see the way Jesus saw when he girded himself with a towel and knelt down to wash the feet of his friends. The Gospel says that Jesus filled his basin that evening as one who knew that he had come from God and that he was going to God. The girl with the foot in her hands is being taught to reverence all that God has given and will again gather up. Rubbing the dampness from the skin of that foot, she is being taught that the God who makes a claim on her is a God who cherishes bodies. She is being taught to honor the body as a holy creation of God, blessed in its strength and fragility, in its smoothness and roughness, in the way it both conceals and reveals who we truly are.

Whenever Jesus patted mud into the eyes of someone who could not see, or touched a leper, or sat at the bedside of the sick and dying, he taught those around him how God sees and honors the body. But in the course of his ministry, he also received care from those who could see as God sees. Once a woman entered a house where Jesus was having supper and began weeping over his feet and wiping them dry with her hair. His host wondered what sort of prophet Jesus could be if he didn't know what sort of woman this was, if he would allow himself to be touched by a woman whose long, loose hair announced her sin. And when Mary of

Pondering the Mystery of the Body

Bethany poured out a pound of perfume and rubbed it into Jesus' feet, Judas Iscariot was scandalized by what he believed to be the waste of resources. But these women did not see with the eyes of those who despise the bodies of the marginalized nor with the eyes of those for whom value could only be measured in money. They looked on Jesus' body with the eyes of God: they knew how he was made. They remembered he was dust. They knew that he had come from God and that he was going to God. And so they honored his body with perfume and reverenced his body's fragility with tears.

This is our task also: to learn to see our bodies and the bodies of others through the eyes of God. To learn to see the body as both fragile and deeply blessed. To remember the body's vulnerability and to rejoice in the body as a sign of God's gracious bounty.

Chapter 3

BATHING
THE
BODY

———

My best friend, Kay, recently gave her mother, who is dying of cancer, her last bath in a tub.

Both my friend and her mother, Thelma, love to bathe and have made a long, delicious ritual of it. Kay's earliest memory is of sitting on the bathroom floor each night, talking with her mother during her mother's night-time bath. After a long day of teaching kindergarten and engaging her own three active daughters, Thelma would step into the tub, prop her head up in back, and relax into the water. "I was eye level with her," Kay remembers, "her body the mirror image of mine, simply twenty-seven years older."

Kay and her mother would talk about this and that, my friend making sure, while she had her to herself in the damp, warm intimacy of the bathroom, to tell her mother everything she had been unable to tell her during the day. Thelma would listen and comment as she washed herself with a cloth, swishing water over her right arm and then over her left. Finally, she would wring out her washcloth, shake it open, close her eyes, and scrub her face with it until it shone pink. Kay would hand her a towel and watch as her mother dried herself off, smoothed on face cream, and welcomed her husband into the bathroom for his bath. Kay went off to bed listening to her parents' voices rise and fall through the sound of running water.

Since her earliest days, Kay has given delighted attention to her mother's every gesture and applied herself to the imitation of them. I have seen my friend wring out *her* washcloth and scrub her face pink a hundred times at least. And now that her mother is dying of non-Hodgkin's lymphoma, the attention Kay brings to her mother has only intensified. Like the little girl in the bathroom, she continues to study her beautiful mother as if her mother's body were the most sacred of texts. And, as always, her loving attention is rewarded. Just as her mother had taught her how to turn a bath into a time of quiet pleasure and intimacy, she now teaches my friend how to die. It is her mother's last, great gift to her.

Thelma is living her last days. Her family surrounds her. Kay writes to me of her mother's last bath.

> She insists on being clean,
> and today Amy and I invited her to a bath
> if she was up to it
> in the late afternoon.

The appointed time came.
Mom worked and worked and finally sat up
on the side of her bed,
legs down
feet toward the floor.
Then the vomiting began,
violent vomiting taking her last bit of strength.

She told me to draw her bath
showing me with her hands how deep.
I turned the bathroom heater on.
I cleaned the hair out of the drain trap.
I ran all hot water at first to warm the tub
then moderated it, checking with my wrist.

She shuffled to the bathroom,
sat down on a towel I had placed on the edge of the
    tub.
We undressed her.
She stood up, grabbed the grip bar that dad had
    installed for her.
I stood behind her, straddling the tub,
ready to catch her
in case she fell.
She told me I needed to trust her
to know what she could do.

And then
that precious body that I have looked at and loved
    and
memorized
lowered into the water.
She never opened her eyes
lay there
still
silent

Bathing the Body

then put her hand out and I placed a plastic cup in it
as we had discussed I would.
She slowly lifted a cup of water
and poured it over her arms.
Lying back down
she poured another cup over her throat and neck
sighing a tiny sound of pleasure.
The water sounded like baptism
holy, quiet, small splashes.

The bath ended with Kay pouring cup after cup of water onto her mother's head, gently moving her fingers through the tiny bit of hair still growing there. Thelma kept both ears shut against the water with the pointer finger of each hand. Her quiet sighs of pleasure were matched by the sobs rising up from inside my friend as her tears fell into the water of her mother's last bath.

The eyes of love with which Kay gazes at her dying mother perceive the sacredness of every inch of her mother's suffering body. This does not mean that her heart is not breaking. This does not mean that it is not unbearable to hold her mother as she vomits, to watch helplessly as she struggles to swallow even one sip of water. This does not mean that Kay does not hate the death her mother is dying. It means that when her mother pours water over her throat and neck, my friend can hear the echo of the waters of her mother's baptism, which promises that her dignity will not be compromised by bedsores or vomit. It means that no matter how wasted her mother's body becomes, she recognizes there what the women who washed Jesus' feet with tears and ointment saw: a suffering temple of the Holy Spirit, cherished by God.

The Pleasures of the Bath

In the beginning, we dwell in water. We grow in it, and once outside our mother's womb, water continues to keep us alive, washing our every cell. We are bathed inside and out by this life-giving substance of which both we and the earth are mostly made. Bathing is one of the first and most basic ways we honor our bodies. Few other daily acts bring us into such close proximity with our nakedness and vulnerability. Few other daily acts require us to touch our bodies so intimately. Few other daily acts allow us to mark the transitions in our days more completely. Few other daily acts offer our bodies such immediate comfort.

Why is bathing such a comfort to us? From what does bathing draw its power? Perhaps bathing returns us to our beginnings in water. Perhaps water awakens our body's own deep memory of—and gratitude for—its first home. Diane Ackerman, author of *A Natural History of the Senses,* notes that we have the ancient Egyptians—"a clean, ingeniously sybaritic people obsessed with hygiene" —to thank for the practice of bathing. "[T]hey invented the sumptuous art of the bath—an art that might be restorative, sensuous, religious, or calming, depending on one's mood." Surely the power of that sumptuous art lies in the hope of rebirth that resonates within the body's memory of its earliest beginnings.

The comforts of bathing are well known. From a shower first thing in the morning, to a sponge bath when we're sick in bed, to a (however infrequent) long soak in a tub, bathing can bring us back to life. Of course, like all other bodily pleasures, the pleasures of the bath have been highly commodified. Whole stores—indeed, whole chains of stores—exist to sell products intended to increase the pleasure of bathing: scented soaps and lotions, special sponges, candles to illuminate the tub. The large, well-appointed bathroom has become a symbol of wealth and well-being. Custom-made shower fittings, oversized, Jacuzzi-jetted tubs, and heated towel racks have come to define a version of the good life that is out of reach for many of us. But does an accumulation of such products heighten the pleasures of the bath, or might they overwhelm and obscure them? It is certainly possible to practice bathing as an expensive pastime. But often the simplest baths are the most renewing.

Some of my best bathing memories are of kneeling at troughs with other dusty, tired young people, washing our hands, face, arms, and legs before falling into bed in youth hostels across Europe. Accustomed as I was to hot showers in private, I despaired at first when I saw those troughs. But I learned to revel in those baths, in sharing with others the delicious feeling of scrubbing hands, face, and feet clean after a day of tromping through train stations and meadows, cathedrals and back roads.

Many men I know use their baths as a way to move

from one part of their day to another. One friend has told me how much he loves his morning shower, loves the way it helps him emerge from sleep and get ready to greet his daughters when they awake. Another friend's husband works with his hands as a carpenter and saves his bath for the end of his workday. Bathing is the way he prepares himself to be with his family in the evenings. He washes off the dust of the day and joins his family unencumbered.

My sister is a great lover of baths, perhaps because she was so often denied the pleasure of them as a child suffering from severe skin allergies. Because water threatened to further dry her cracked and broken skin, my mother often gave my sister waterless baths by rubbing her with creams and gently wiping them off with a soft cloth.

As she grew older, her skin began to tolerate water, and my sister turned to baths for comfort. Before the birth of her son, when she began to go into labor, she immediately filled her tub with warm water and lowered herself into it, laboring for the first few hours supported and surrounded by water. When the pain put her beyond the reach of water's comforts, she went to the hospital, where she learned that her labor had progressed too far for her to receive any pain medication. She asked the midwife for a stool, sat down on it in the shower, and rode out the worst of her labor with water drumming a steady rhythm on her belly. My nephew made his way into the world through a body solaced by water.

So powerful is the body's response to bathing that

"taking the waters" in spas around the world has long been credited with the healing of a variety of ailments. Hot springs from Japan to Germany have attracted visitors seeking the therapy of bathing in hot water bubbling up from the earth itself. From all over the world, people travel to the American Southwest and to the Dead Sea for mud baths believed to heal and regenerate the skin. But bathing has been practiced to renew not only the body but the mind as well. Perhaps you've had the experience of having a solution to a problem come to you, unbidden, in the shower. Diane Ackerman notes that Benjamin Franklin brought the first bathtub to the United States in the 1780s and loved to retreat to the tub to write and think. Ackerman herself has a pine plank that she lays across her tub so that she can write in the bath. "In the bath, water displaces much of your weight, and you feel light, your blood pressure drops. When the water temperature and the body temperature converge, my mind lifts free and travels by itself. One summer, lolling in baths, I wrote an entire verse play. . . . "

Bathing stimulates not only healing and creativity but sexual pleasure as well. The Bible bears witness to this: it is when David, walking on the roof of his palace, catches sight of Bathsheba bathing that he becomes intent on seducing her (2 Samuel 11:2). Bathing can be very sexy, and no special soaps or shower fixtures are needed to make it so.

And what a very deep pleasure it is to bathe with a beloved. Bathing gentles our touch, makes us tender and attentive. Elizabeth Bishop ends a poem celebrating the long, black hair of her lover with this invitation: "Come, let me wash it in this big, tin basin, battered and shiny like the moon." How better to attend to the body of the beloved than to lather and rinse, caress and admire it in a bath?

"I must confess," wrote Henry David Thoreau in his journal, "[that] there is nothing so strange to me as my own body—I love any other piece of nature, almost, better." Bathing is one way to overcome that strangeness, one way to acquaint and reacquaint ourselves with our bodies, to greet our bodies each day. The pleasures of the bath remind us how much simple daily acts of care matter, how they help shape, over time, our feelings about the body. It matters whether we bathe a child attentively or distractedly, gently or roughly. It matters if we understand ourselves to be caring for our body when we bathe. It matters whether and how we help bathe the bodies of the sick and dying.

Even as Thelma's body deteriorated, even as its operations slipped from her control, she still longed to care for her body by taking a bath. She was fortunate to have someone nearby who knew her bathing habits and could help her have the bath she wanted. Kay knew how to offer such care to her mother because she had learned over the years what a good bath requires. She knew to turn on the bathroom heater. She knew to clean the hair from the drain. She knew to warm the tub with hot water first before moderating the temperature. She knew these things because she had been bathed with care by her mother as a child and because she had been invited, night after night, into her mother's own bath ritual. She had learned in the course of everyday life that the body is worthy of such attention, that we ought to make time to care for our bodies in this way, that when the body is bathed with gentleness the whole person is soothed and renewed. Thelma had taught her daughter to bring extraordinary perception to an ordinary activity, so that when it was time for her mother's last bath, my friend could see in the water the reflection of the body's holiness and hear in its quiet splashing the promises of God.

CLEANLINESS IS NEXT TO GODLINESS

In our everyday lives, of course, we bathe most often not to feel sexy or creative or to endure great pain, but simply to get clean. Getting clean is only deceptively simple, however. In many religious traditions, cleanliness is not just a matter of a well-scrubbed body but also of holiness.

In the law codes of the Hebrew Bible, bathing is required to restore an unclean person to cleanness. Persons could be rendered unclean in many ways, often through natural, unavoidable processes. (Uncleanness that resulted from human choices, such as adultery and homicide, was more difficult to repair.) Men who had a discharge from their penises were considered unclean, as were menstruating women, those who had come into contact with a corpse, and those who had come into contact with blood. Such uncleanness could be remedied by temporarily separating oneself from the community and by performing particular ritual actions, including bathing. Through bathing, those whose uncleanness compromised their proximity to the holy could be restored to the community and to God.

The law codes of the Hebrew Bible also require bathing as preparation for worship and meals. God commanded that the priests of the community bathe before putting on the holy vestments and wash their hands and feet before entering the tent of meeting or approaching the altar. Everyone was required to wash before every meal. In this way, not just worship but ordinary activities such as eating became occasions to remember that one's life is sustained by the gifts of a gracious God, gifts that one must prepare oneself, body and soul, to receive.

But the prophets remind us that bathing alone is not enough to restore us to God. Whenever God's people failed to care for the most vulnerable among them, the prophets rebuked them, often drawing on the language of the bath. "Though you wash yourself with lye and use much soap, the stain of your guilt is still before me, says the Lord God," Jeremiah roars (Jeremiah 2:22). "Wash yourself," God commands in Isaiah, "make yourselves clean" (Isaiah 1:16). "O Jerusalem, wash your heart clean of wickedness so that you may be saved" (Jeremiah 4:14). If only we could rinse away intolerance, hatefulness, and evil motivations with a bath. But a change of heart—that more difficult operation—is always required as well. The Hebrew Bible reminds us that although bathing is not a magical act, it can be an act that prepares for that change

Bathing the Body

of heart through the heightening of our attention to God and one another.

Bathing gives physical expression to the longing to be washed by God in a bath that heals and cleanses, changes and renews. "Wash me thoroughly from my iniquity," the psalmist famously wrote, "and cleanse me from my sin. Purge me with hyssop, and I shall be clean, wash me, and I shall be whiter than snow" (Psalm 51:2, 7). By marking every meal, every act of worship, every attempt to restore oneself to right relationship with God and the community by bathing the body or at least some parts of it, God's people expressed with their bodies their desire to be holy and their recognition that they must always be starting over, always beginning again.

Writer Kathleen Norris reminds us that "reluctance to care for the body is one of the first symptoms of extreme melancholia. . . . Shampooing the hair, washing the body, brushing the teeth, drinking enough water, taking a daily vitamin, going for a walk, as simple as they seem, are acts of self-respect. They enhance one's ability to take pleasure in oneself and in the world. . . . Care is not passive— the word derives from an Indo-European word meaning 'to cry out,' as in a lament. Care asserts that as difficult and painful as life can be, it is worth something to be in the present, alive, doing one's daily bit."

Thinking of bathing as an affirmation of the goodness of life even in the face of life's inevitable pain might help us reinterpret the old saying "Cleanliness is next to godliness." Did your parents ever employ this familiar saying to respond to a reluctance to wash your hands before dinner or take a bath before bed? In such a context, the phrase can be moderately annoying or amusing (depending on your mood); in others, it can be dangerously destructive. When it is used to define some people as "unclean" and far from God because of illness, race, religion, or sexual orientation, it places them outside of the care of the community. Perhaps, however, the notion that cleanliness is next to godliness is not a call to divide the world into the clean and the unclean, but rather an acknowledgment that when we care for our bodies we respond to God's desire to see all creation thrive. Caring for the needs of our bodies, we choose life over and over again.

Attention to our bodies through the simple act of bathing might also remind us of the mystery that our bodies somehow reflect the divine image. Jewish midrash tells a story of the beloved sage Hillel, who, on his way to the bathhouse, explained to his disciples that he was going to carry out a *mitzvah,* a commandment. "Is it a religious obligation to bathe?" they asked. "Yes," replied Hillel, "If the statues of kings erected in theatres and circuses are regularly scoured and washed by the person appointed to look after them, how much more I, who has been created in God's image and likeness."

Bathing also allows us to honor the image of God in others, as my friend did when she helped her mother enjoy a last bath, as members of foot-washing churches do every time they kneel before one another, towel in hand. St. Benedict, the author of the most widely used rule for monastic life, mandated washing the feet of all who visited the monastery as a way of adoring Christ in

Bathing the Body

every guest, especially "poor people and pilgrims, because in them more particularly Christ is received." One of the most visible ways early monastic communities welcomed Christ in every guest was to bathe their hands and feet: "The abbot shall pour water on the hands of the guests, and the abbot with the entire community shall wash their feet. After the washing they will recite this verse: 'God, we have received your mercy in the midst of your temple'" (Psalm 47 [48]:10).

Bathing another—a lover, a child, a stranger, a friend—allows us to reverence the image of God in the bodies of others. And learning to see that image in bodies that are well or ill, scarred or whole, like or unlike our own, is mercy indeed.

A friend of mine learned how bathing could be used to adore the image of God present in herself and others from her father when she was a teenager with a face marked by acne. She remembers a day when her anguish over the appearance of her face made her feel unable to leave the house. Seeing her distress, her father asked if he could help by teaching her a new way to bathe. Leading her to the bathroom, he leaned over the sink and splashed water over his face, telling her, "On the first splash, say 'In the name of the Father,' on the second, 'in the name of the Son,' and on the third, 'in the name of the Holy Spirit.' Then look up into the mirror and remember that you are a child of God, full of grace and beauty." Her father's gift has persisted throughout my friend's life. She integrated her father's reverence for the reflection of the divine in the body into her own daughters' bath time, making each bath a baptismal act. While they washed, they sang blessings over each part of their bodies, remembering that they were children of God, made in God's image.

THE CHRISTIAN WATER-BATH

The Christian practice of honoring the body begins with bathing because Christian life itself begins with a bath. For Christians, every bath is an opportunity to remember the waters of our baptism, our immersion into the death and Resurrection of Christ, our initiation into the household of God. With every bath, we have an opportunity to recall our truest self, our most authentic identity. With every bath, we might, through attention to the mystery of our body as formed in the image of God, gain perspective on God's image in all of life.

The bath of baptism gathers up the tension between sacredness and vulnerability, for baptism is not a pleasant soak in a tub but an immersion in death. As anyone who has ever felt the pull of an ocean undertow knows, water not only has the power to support and comfort us, it has the power to destroy us as well. Waters that close over our head might never open again. Naked and unguarded, we are vulnerable when we bathe.

When I was nine years old, I joined my church by being examined by my minister before the congregation at the end of the Sunday morning service and by being baptized at a service later that afternoon. During the morning service I was asked by Mr. Wallace, my minister, "Do you believe that Jesus is the Christ, the son of the living God, and do you accept him as your Lord and Savior?" I answered yes, happily believing in things unseen yet reflected in the loving faces of my family and my church. This was a wonderful, warm moment for me, a moment when I felt the love of God in the love of my community, when I felt supported in the mysterious matter of "having faith."

The baptism itself was a very different sort of experience, however. Dressed in my white choir robe, I walked down four or five steps into the warm water of the baptismal pool to be welcomed with a smile by my minister. As we had practiced, I placed my hands on Mr. Wallace's arm, and he gently covered my nose and mouth with a handkerchief. Here again was the love of God reflected in a person who loved me. But when he lowered me into the water, like a dancer dipping his partner, the faces and voices of my minister and my church disappeared and I was completely immersed—in water, in darkness, in a kind of roaring silence. Unlike the girl who had confidently professed her faith that morning, I felt, under the water, out of control, in the presence, perhaps, of the living God who is always more mysterious, more unknowable than even the most compelling of our affirmations can say. And although I could not have articulated it then, I was most certainly in the presence of my own inevitable death, even as I was immersed in waters that promised more life. After Mr. Wallace pulled me up

HONORING THE BODY

out of the water, I was disoriented enough to need another adult to lead me, dripping, up the steps that led out.

That night, as I lay in bed, I wondered over the difference between the ease of answering Mr. Wallace's questions in the morning and the unsettling experience of going under in the afternoon. Not only did the great water-bath welcome me into the household of God, it also set before me the work of a lifetime: the endless reaching out for God from the frail bridge of language, the endless listening for God's voice in darkness and in light, in silence and in words, the endless struggle with the frequent discomfort of God's claims on us.

Early accounts of baptism give some sense of the terrors of submitting to its waters. The baptism Jesus himself experienced, along with many others, was a baptism in the living water of the Jordan River, administered by a strange, wild man who had been living in the wilderness, surviving on insects, clothing himself in animal hair (Mark 1:1–11). The baptism that the great Christian teacher St. Augustine would have experienced in the fourth century was no doubt unnerving as well. Although administered not by a wild stranger but by his beloved bishop Ambrose, and performed not in a rushing river but in the baptistry of the cathedral in Milan, it would have been awesome all the same, taking place in the night of the Easter Vigil. Like other new Christians that evening, men and women of all ages, Augustine would have descended, alone and completely naked, into a deep pool of water. Ambrose would have met him there and would have held him by the shoulders, three times, beneath a gushing fountain. Augustine would have moved from the nakedness of his baptism to being clothed in a white robe, from his solitary descent under the water into the community of Christians, from the darkness of the baptistry into a basilica flooded with light. Going under the waters, naked and alone, must have made rising into community and light all the more wondrous.

Any time we take off our clothes and immerse ourselves in water or stand under a shower, the sound of the spray in our ears blocking out all other sounds, we are vulnerable. In the bath of baptism, we encounter the most radical sign of our body's vulnerability—that we are mortal, that we will one day die. In baptism, however, our death is joined to Christ's death, our life to Christ's life. The waters of baptism wash away everything that obscures the sacredness inherent in the vulnerability of our bodies. In the bath of baptism, it is our vulnerability itself that is clothed in a mercy that can never be removed.

Along with the tension between sacredness and vulnerability, baptism also gathers up the tension between the integrity of our bodies and our bodies in relation to others, as I learned during my daughter's baptism. In my own denomination, we do not baptize babies, believing that each person should choose baptism consciously, prayerfully. My husband is Roman Catholic, a tradition that does baptize babies, believing that God's gift of grace, freely given in baptism, is available to all without exception, that even a tiny infant can be clothed in the garments of faith. In our premarriage counseling, years ago, I remember the priest asking us whether or not we would have any baby that we might conceive baptized as an infant. As we (for whom the idea of having a child seemed too alien to imagine) stumbled around looking for an answer, he laughed and said that if we didn't, my husband's mother would probably just sneak off to the bathroom and do it herself! I loved the thought of my future mother-in-law leaning over the bathroom sink with her precious grandchild, whispering a baptismal blessing as she scooped water, three times, over the baby's head.

So when we did decide to become parents, we also had to decide about baptism. We each saw the good in the other's tradition more clearly than we could see the good in our own, with me arguing for a Catholic baptism and my husband arguing for letting the child choose baptism (or not) for herself later on. But once our daughter was born, once we had beheld the mystery and beauty of her, we found ourselves longing for a ritual to welcome her and give thanks for her and seal her as God's own beloved child. So we gathered our friends and family and did both of what our traditions do when a child is born. My father, a minister in the Christian Church (Disciples of Christ) dedicated our daughter to God and us to the task of caring for her with words of quiet eloquence. My friend Kay, also a Disciples minister, prayed that we would, in every gesture, invite our daughter into the divine mystery that is at the heart of all life. Another dear friend, a Passionist priest, baptized her. It was a Disciples dedication and Catholic baptism, all in one. Members one

Bathing the Body

of another, we enveloped her in the practices of both of our traditions.

My daughter's baptism was a day of incredible happiness for me. We sang songs about the inexhaustible mystery of God and the blessings of a life lived immersed in that mystery. One friend read the story of Jesus' own baptism in the Jordan; another read a passage from Jeremiah about God's promise to write a living word, full of presence, on the text of our hearts. Our daughter slept until the first note of the first song and then awoke, solemn and attentive, seeming to understand that something important was happening. My father and my best friend dedicated her and prayed over her in words rich and true. And just before our friend, dressed in white robe and stole, baptized her in the waters of life, our daughter reached out her hand and tugged at his sleeve. As another friend said to me afterwards, it was as if she were saying, "I *choose* this, I *want* this."

As our friend poured water three times over her precious head, my daughter's eyes locked on the eyes of her godmother, who, truth be told, had argued against the baptism. Kay coveted for my daughter a memory of the awesome moment of complete immersion that we both carry inside us. I could see in the fierce gaze that they held between them my daughter's recognition of my friend as someone to cling to and my friend's commitment to pass on to my daughter everything she knows about life with God. I knew in that moment that we had offered our daughter the very best of what we had: baptism and dedication, music and scripture, argument and prayer, and family and friends who would wrap her round with the stories and struggles of faith. I imagined then, with fervent hope, a long life for my daughter, undergirded by this day, this moment.

In the midst of my profound satisfaction, however, I felt a vague tug of sadness. The very aspect of baptism that gave me such hope for my daughter—that of being received into a community whose members had pledged to accompany her through a life of faith—was precisely what caused me to grieve a little. For we had now acknowledged in public that our five-month-old daughter belonged not only to the integrity of our little family of three but to a much larger community as well. She belonged to a church that was mine and to a church that was not mine. She belonged to the trinity of godparents she is blessed to have. She belonged to the God who gave her life and would one day gather up her life again. She was not mine alone.

But her baptism did not just mark her self in relation to others, it also marked the beautiful integrity, fierce and solitary, of her truest, most authentic self. It marked a self that, clothed in strength and mercy, will be called upon by faith to embrace the claims of others for justice, love, and respect and to resist the claims of those who would exploit and harm. As she leaned backwards toward the bowl of shining baptismal water, eyes locked on her godmother's eyes, I saw a child blessed with family and friends who would honor her self in relation and her self alone. I saw a small body beautiful in its separateness and in its deep connection with others. And as the priest carefully bathed her in water that is both death and life, I sang holy, holy, holy in my heart to a God in whose image our integral, relational bodies are somehow mysteriously formed.

Chapter 4

CLOTHING THE BODY

———

In baptism, we are not only bathed but also clothed. "As many of you as were baptized into Christ have clothed yourselves with Christ," writes Paul in his letter to the Galatians. In baptism we are clothed in our true identity as children of God, an identity deeper even than our ethnicity, our social status, our gender: "There is no longer Jew or Greek, there is no longer slave or free, there is no longer male or female; for all of you are one in Christ Jesus" (Galatians 3:27–29).

The trouble is, in this broken and struggling world, whether our bodies are honored or dishonored is usually not based on a recognition of our true identity as God's own children, but precisely on our ethnicity, our social status, our gender. We may all be one in Christ Jesus, but the long history of damage done to Jewish bodies, enslaved bodies, and female bodies simply because they were Jewish, enslaved, or female (or black, or homosexual, or disabled, or too young to protect themselves) gathers to a scream that threatens to drown out Paul's revolutionary words. The fact that a portion of that damage has been done by Christians, sometimes in the name of the one in whom they were clothed at baptism, testifies to the ways in which baptismal garb, though invisible, can become stained beyond recognition.

Those clothed in the garments of Christ are called to clothe others. When you clothe those who are naked and unprotected, Jesus said, you clothe me. My friend Susan remembers her church's attempt to clothe a refugee family from Cambodia when she was a child. A man from the congregation stood before his brothers and sisters in Christ and asked them to provide clothing for the family. He asked them to help clothe children getting ready to enter a new school and parents about to look for jobs that could support their new life in the United States.

A few weeks later, this man stood before the congregation again, speaking in a quiet voice that was nevertheless vibrating with anger. "I asked you to *clothe* this family," he said to those assembled. "Instead I have received castoffs from decades ago, clothes that are out of date, out of style. Clothes that are missing buttons, clothes with broken zippers, clothes that are in some cases *dirty*. These are not the kinds of clothes a man can find a job in. You would never send your children to school dressed in the clothes you have offered to this family. I am not asking for your castoffs. *I am asking you to clothe this family.*"

This man knew that clothes could offer protection for vulnerable people in need. And he believed that those clothed in the garments of Christ should know better than to offer clothes that would offer no such protection, clothes that could even increase vulnerability. Because of his willingness to bear witness to what Christ calls us to when he calls us to clothe our neighbors, that congregation had an opportunity to think about the relationship between their baptismal garments and the clothes in their overstuffed closets. And they had an opportunity to try again to clothe the Christ who had asked for their help.

CLOTHES MAKE THE (WO)MAN

I recently heard one of my students, who grew up in an Amish community and wore the Amish garb until her graduation from college and her entrance into the more liberal Mennonite Church, preach a beautiful sermon in which she reflected on the story of Peter's denial of Jesus. Musing on how something had caused others to recognize Peter as a disciple, my student confessed to a nagging worry. "Now that I don't wear clothing that marks me as [a] member of a Christian community," she said, "is there anything about me that says I have been with Jesus?"

What marks us as children of God? Can our clothing bear witness to our commitments and our truest selves? Can the daily clothing of our bodies illuminate our invisible baptismal garb? And if bathing can heighten our attention to the mystery of our bodies and to our creation in God's image, might the clothing of our bodies do the same?

People in every age have sought to illuminate who they really are through clothing and adorning the body. Just as we live in the tension of being a body and having a body, feeling sometimes that we are our bodies and at other times as if we simply wear our bodies like a garment of skin that covers our true self, we human beings seem to have a great desire to wear clothes and adornments that do more than just cover our nakedness. We want our clothing to express something important about us. Not only do we *have* clothes, we are, in some sense, defined by our clothes. "Clothes make the man," as the old saying goes.

Some express their deepest commitments through the refusal of adornment. The Old Order Amish wear their commitment to simplicity on their bodies in their plain clothes, unadorned even by buttons. Others, like the medieval abbess Hildegard of Bingen, who often adorned her nuns in jewels that she believed reflected interior spiritual gifts, invest every button with meaning. Those in mourning often wear black, allowing their clothes to speak their grief to the world. My friend, Kay, who is losing her mother to cancer, believes that black also signifies, *Watch out. I've lost my beloved and I am angry. Don't mess with me.* In the Bible, grief and repentance are sometimes articulated in clothes of sackcloth and a head smeared with dirt and ashes and sometimes in clothes that are ripped and torn. When Reuben finds that his brother Joseph has been sold into slavery, he tears his clothes frantically, helplessly (Genesis 37:29). We wear our clothes as extensions of our bodies and as signs of what is happening invisibly inside of us.

Clothing can also be used to prepare for and mark a change in our lives. Brides and grooms adorn themselves gloriously in order to ready themselves for the moment when they will speak their radical promises to one another. My college always holds a clothing ceremony prior to graduation, during which graduates are clothed in their graduation robe by someone important to them. When my sister slipped my robe on over my shoulders and fastened the hooks with her beautiful hands, I felt myself putting on a new life the shape of which I couldn't yet imagine. When Francis of Assisi, the son of a wealthy cloth merchant, heard the voice of God calling him to a life of poverty, he unclothed himself before his raging father. The simple brown habit he afterwards wore expressed his interior commitments, just as, later, the wounds that appeared on his body marked his devotion to the suffering Christ.

Clothing can yield up a surprising amount of information; ask any teenager. In my high school, brand names, style of clothes, and certain color combinations distinguished preppies from potheads from jocks. How important it was to us all to dress in a way that identified us with the security of a particular group, even those who considered themselves least bound by the requirements of fashion. Preppies dressed in relentlessly cheerful pastel pinks and greens that spoke of satisfaction with the way things were. Potheads (and other kids on the margins) wore flannel shirts and jeans, dark colors, and dark makeup. The high school massacre in Littleton, Colorado, has called the nation's attention to the way clothing marks off social groups in a school, and disaffected kids dressed in black across the country have endured intense suspicion in its aftermath. Tom Beaudoin, both a member and a student of Generation X, reads the Gothic look of many of these kids as a sign not of hostility but of grief. For him, black clothes and dark circles penciled around the eyes mark an attempt to master suffering by dressing ironically in the colors of mourning.

But, of course, it is not just teenagers who seek to wear their identities on their bodies; adults do as well, and just as often. I've frequently heard middle-aged athletes in my South Side neighborhood, for example, comparing their clothes with those worn by other athletes. In Chicago, athletes on the South Side pride themselves on dressing simply for biking and running on the lakefront, in comparison with their North Side counterparts, who are distinguished (to South Siders, at least) by their unnecessarily expensive equipment and dress.

Body adornments that go beyond clothing that can be put on and taken off, into the more permanent realms of body piercing, tattooing, and scarring, are popular, particularly among young people. These "body projects," as historian Joan Brumberg calls them, turn the body itself into a canvas to be painted with one's identity, a page to be inscribed with bodily experience. Web sites of those enthusiastic about body piercing suggest that having one's eyebrow, lip, tongue, navel, or genitals pierced is a way of claiming alternative space in the culture, of setting oneself apart from the mainstream. (Of course, once fashion designers, super models, and pop stars pick up the trend, the alternative begins to move inexorably *into* the mainstream.)

Brumberg, who has devoted considerable attention to the body projects of American girls across several generations, believes contemporary body piercing is the inevitable outcome of "the pared-down, segmented, increasingly exposed, part-by-part orientation to the female body." By wounding and marking each part, our culture's relentless, evaluative gaze is permanently inscribed on the body. She sees another recent clothing trend, that of wearing underwear as outerwear, as further eroding the distinction between public and private and reflecting a profound confusion about intimacy that is dangerous for young women. (Interestingly, because young women talk about having their genitals pierced as a way of creating an erotic secret that they share only with their boyfriends, she also sees genital piercing as a way of claiming some private space "in a world where the body has been made public.")

Tom Beaudoin has a different take on piercing and tattooing, one that takes into account the religious yearnings of those seeking to mark their bodies. "Piercing," he argues, "signifies immediate, bodily, and constant attention to the intimacy of experience." Piercing and tattooing serve to bring interior wounds to the surface of the body and to bring sustained attention to the body itself. For him, this is the attention not of a culture transmitting its impossible expectations for the body but of those whose deepest experiences are oriented toward the body. For Beaudoin, navel piercing in particular indicates the exposure of the person's center and invites others to "navel gaze," to reflect on their own center of self.

Piercing and tattooing also reflect, for Beaudoin, the failure of contemporary institutions—most notably the church—to provide experiences that are deeply meaningful and so deeply marking. All of these trends in bodily adornment he reads as shot through with Generation X's desire for meaning, for God. He interprets the trend of wearing underwear as outerwear as reflecting a desire for "intimate disclosure, intimate association, intimation revelation." For Beaudoin, the same desire marks pierced and tattooed bodies as well.

For some people, however, marking the body is a sign of having had a deeply marking experience rather than a sign of their desire for one. When asked about her tattoo, the novelist Darcey Steinke said she got it to honor the person she had become after a time of great sadness: "I had had a bad year, marriage trouble and just a lot of sadness and I felt like I was different than I had been, transformed, and I wanted to honor this with a tattoo. So I had a friend who's a stained glass artist do a design and I got the tattoo two years ago. I have not regretted it for one minute ever."

HONORING THE BODY

FREEDOM AND CONSTRAINT REVISITED

My mother, who came of age in the years before girls began piercing their tongues, does, however, have two tiny scars on her ears from the day her older sister and a friend numbed them with ice cubes and pierced them with a needle. My mother had let the holes grow over long before I was born, but the two scars still mark her ears.

My mother asked me to wait until I was eighteen to decide whether or not to have my ears pierced. Naturally, I did not understand this (although, being afraid of pain, I was secretly grateful for the impediment of her disapproval). But even though I longed to be able to wear pierced earrings, I waited. Eventually, during my first year of college, a dorm mate took me to a glassy mall, where a man pierced my ears, not with ice and a needle, but with a gun that spit earrings. I had to keep two awkward-looking gold-plated studs in my ears for six weeks, cleaning them with alcohol and turning them twice a day, and then, finally, I could wear the long, dangly earrings I had long coveted.

Eighteen years later, I now understand why my mother discouraged me from having my ears pierced. For I have grown tired of adorning my ears. Of course, during the years when I thought my choice of earrings said something important about who I was, the really good earrings were always pierced, never clip-ons. You never saw in the clip-on section any wonderful, dangly earrings of feathers and stone that would announce you as a sensitive, poetic young woman. But over the years I have lost interest. I have gone from wearing long, dangly earrings, to smaller, painted earrings, to two tiny sapphires (a birthday gift from my husband). My daughter lost the sapphires during one of her rampages through my jewelry box, now filled mostly with old ID cards and single members of formerly two-earring sets, so I have now quit wearing earrings altogether. I give some thought now and then to going out to find some new earrings I might like to wear, but I don't ever seem to get around to it. I see now that I will, like my mother, be marked by a small scar, a shadow, on each earlobe.

My mother, I realize now with all the wisdom of hindsight, resisted my early requests to have my ears pierced because she wanted me to be unencumbered, free from having to wear earrings every day. It was one of the many ways she tried to teach me to hold nonessential things lightly so that I would have the strength to hold tight to what is important. And although it is admittedly a small thing, I do feel encumbered by these holes in my ears, mainly because I know I look like I forgot to put on my earrings. So I try to regard them as marks of the girl I was, innocuous marks she left on my body on her way to being an adult more interested in paring down than in committing to additional adornment.

But that's just me, of course. My idea of a great vacation is to be able to wear exactly the same clothes every day, pausing only to wash them once in a while. I would love to have fewer choices about adornment cluttering up my day. For me, freedom of choice has become constraining, the time spent shopping or deciding what to wear a frustration.

Other people revel in the choices for clothing and adorning their bodies, finding the freedom delicious and rewarding. Some people, let's face it, just know how to wear their clothes. This has nothing to do with having a particular body shape. I know plenty of women and men, of all shapes and sizes, who wear their clothes (and their earrings) like Cleopatra. They look great, and they're a delight to gaze upon. The writer Daniel Mendelsohn writes of his classics teacher: "She was so emphatically herself that she forced you, by the very fact of herself, her presence, her jewels and cigarettes and intellect, to react, to be yourself, to think." For some people, adornment *is* an extension of who they are and it *does* express something important about them, so that even jewelry gets gathered up into the force of their personality, becoming a part of it, adding to it.

If we are to honor our bodies, it is important to pay attention to how adornment frees or constrains us. What is constraining for one person can be freeing for another. Whereas tattooing may seem a violation of one's freedom not to be wounded and permanently marked for one person, it might be a gesture of freedom for another. But some clothing trends promise freedom while keeping silent about the ways they constrain. Distinguishing what binds us from what sets us loose to be ourselves is not always easy.

Joan Brumberg tells a story about her students in

the women's history classes she teaches that illustrates what I mean. Studying the lives of girls and women in the nineteenth century, her students, dressed comfortably in sweatshirts and jeans, lamented the constraining girdles and corsets worn by women of the previous century. As the conversation moved to contemporary life, however, the subject of pubic hair removal came up. It's necessary, her students insisted, so that you can feel confident at the beach. Brumberg was amazed that these young women, with all their freedoms, felt such a need to "strictly police their bodies." The greater freedom to bare their bodies on the beach brought with it a set of anxieties that not only constrained but also created a market for more body products. "Progress for women," Brumberg notes, "is obviously filled with ambiguities."

Another kind of constraint, a serious violation of freedom relating to clothing, is the reality of sweatshop practices, including child labor, to make many of the clothes we wear. How and with what we adorn ourselves often has implications for the literal freedom of others. Horror stories crop up from time to time: new immigrants to the United States enslaved by those who provided their passage, forced to sew around the clock; children in the third world working long hours in the garment industry for almost no pay, making clothes destined for this country. Enslavement to the commodification of adornment makes this other, more terrible slavery possible. God intends for all of us to be free. The practice of honoring the body requires habits of adornment that make us vigilant about the effects our choices have on others.

"Is not life more than food and the body more than clothing?" Jesus asks in Matthew's Gospel. Like my mother, wishing me to be unencumbered enough to travel quickly and lightly toward the most important destinations, Jesus urges us toward freedom. "Why do you worry about clothing? Consider the lilies of the field, how they grow; they neither toil nor spin, yet I tell you, even Solomon in all his glory was not clothed like one of these." Are your habits of adornment a burden or a pleasure, a source of anxiety or confidence? Do your clothes free you to be yourself, or do they constrain you by forcing you into an identity that, however fashionable, you would not have chosen? Did the production of your adornments constrain the freedom of another? These are questions that might guide us in our clothing and our adornment, to help us develop our own ideas of what is beautiful, and to allow the daily practice of getting dressed remind us that we are children of a God who desires our freedom.

A Dress Full of Prayers

Several years ago, having miscarried a cherished pregnancy on the day after Christmas, I found myself seemingly screwed to my bed with depression, unable to work, read, or pray.

I was, however, able to talk on the phone. Day after day, I wore out my friends, especially my friend Kay.

Kay had, the year before, left behind job, salary, and colleagues to spend a year in prayer and silence. Violating her dearly bought solitude again and again, I cried to her on the phone, "I am so depressed that I can't even pray. I try to pray, but I can't." A few days later, a package arrived from her that contained a simple beige jumper and a note that read, "I have prayed in this dress every day for a year. You don't have to pray. Just wear it. It is full of prayers."

I did wear that dress. I wore it and wept in it, and cried out *Why?* to God in it. I let the prayers in that dress pray for me when my mouth was dry and full of ashes. And when I became pregnant again, I continued to wear that dress. Kay loves long, loose clothes, and her dress was spacious enough to accompany me nearly to the end of my ninth month. Her prayers were spacious enough, too, to gather up my fear and grief and anger. And my joy, when it came.

I was naked in my grief, and my friend clothed me. Clothing others is a Christian obligation, to be cultivated in every area of our lives. No one must be left naked. I was fortunate enough to participate in a seminar a few years ago that was led by the Mennonite educator Shirley Hershey Showalter. We had gathered to think together about the relationship between our religious lives and our lives as teachers and scholars. Shirley laid out a rich feast of texts for us to consider. But she insisted that we ourselves be the most primary of those texts. Each of us was invited to offer a ten-minute spiritual-intellectual autobiography, so that we would understand how each other's questions and passions had been forged and fired. Shirley was very strict about those ten minutes—she even set an alarm clock that would tell us when our time was about up—but she always allowed ample time for the group to respond to each autobiographical reflection. "We will leave no one standing naked," she insisted. "Everyone who makes herself or himself vulnerable, we will clothe."

When you clothe those who are naked and unprotected, Jesus said, you clothe me. "If a brother or sister is naked and lacks daily food, and one of you says to them, 'Go in peace; keep warm and eat your fill,' and yet you do not supply their bodily needs, what is the good of that?" asks the letter of James. These teachings refer, of course, not to spiritual or psychological nakedness but to literal nakedness—nakedness that is unprotected from cold or heat, rain or wind, or from the gaze of others. The practice of honoring the body includes the clothing of those in need.

The *New York Times* recently reported that "cast-off clothes have become the flotsam of turn-of-the-century affluence. Americans bought 17.2 billion articles of clothing in 1998 . . . and gave [to] the Salvation Army alone several hundred million pieces, well over 100,000 tons." Many of these clothes come to the Salvation Army stained or otherwise beyond repair; these are shredded, bundled into bales, and sold to rag dealers. "Clothes—" said one woman interviewed as she shopped, "I go through them like water."

Many of us go through our clothes like water, adding more and more to our overflowing closets as seasons and fashions change. If you're like me, a portion of those 17.2 billion articles of clothing are hanging askew in your closet or stuffed into the back of your bureau, unworn. My friend Kay has two rules about her clothes. The first is, if it goes unworn for six months, it is taken out, cleaned, pressed, and given away. And the second is like it: when a new article of clothing is purchased, some other article of clothing is donated to someone who needs it. Nothing new comes in without something else going out. In this way, Kay never thinks of any piece of clothing as belonging to herself alone; every shirt, every dress, every coat is destined for someone else. And so she cares for her clothes with that someone else in mind. She keeps them clean, she keeps the buttons tightly fastened, she keeps the zippers repaired, so that when the time comes to give them away, they are in beautiful shape for someone else to enjoy.

There will be times in our lives when we will be called upon to take the coat from our back on the spot and give it to someone in need. But my friend's simple practice is a way of keeping in mind every day our obligation to clothe others, a way of holding those others—whose names we may never know—in our minds and our hearts; it is a daily preparation for giving.

We are called upon to clothe others by a God who clothes us at baptism and offers us again and again, never giving up, the clean, beautiful garments of mercy, justice, and kindness to wear. Because God has compassion for our nakedness, God is a God who clothes. The book of Genesis imagines God making clothes for Adam and

Eve, who had been shamed by the knowledge of their nakedness. The book of Ezekiel describes God clothing Israel, who is imagined as a child abandoned in the wilderness, dirty and naked, her umbilical cord uncut.

> Then I bathed you with water and washed off the blood from you, and anointed you with oil. I clothed you with embroidered cloth and with sandals of fine leather; I bound you in fine linen and covered you with rich fabric. I adorned you with ornaments: I put bracelets on your arms, a chain on your neck, a ring on your nose, earrings in your ears, and a beautiful crown upon your head. . . . Your fame spread among the nations on account of your beauty, for it was perfect because of my splendor that I had bestowed on you, says the Lord God [Ezekiel 16:9–12, 14].

Our nakedness is never beyond the reach of God's desire to clothe and adorn us. Our bodies are never so exposed that we cannot be clothed in the garments that God offers us new in every moment. Kay knew this when she offered her mother a bath during her last days that would echo the bath in which her mother was first clothed in the garments of faith. And Kay's mother knew it as she taught her daughter how to die, how to live in the desire "not to be unclothed but to be further clothed, so that what is mortal may be swallowed up by life" (2 Corinthians 5:4).

Chapter 5

NOURISHING THE BODY

———

In the eastern North Carolina town where I grew up, a celebration demanded a pig roast, or a pig-pickin', as most people called it. Family reunions, graduation parties, wedding rehearsal dinners were often held around the open body of a pig that had been roasted for hours, the meat inside chopped fine, mixed with vinegar, sugar, and spices. North Carolina barbecue. You'd fill your plate with boiled potatoes, cole slaw, and hush puppies, file past the pig cooker, and scoop the barbecue right out of the middle of the pig.

If you are not from North Carolina (or if you keep kosher, or are a committed vegetarian), this may sound appalling. But for those who grew up with what North Carolinians like to think of as Real Barbecue, there's nothing like it. There's a restaurant in my neighborhood in Chicago that claims to specialize in North Carolina barbecue. On any given night it is filled with people who grew up with this food, looking for a bite of something that will taste like the special occasions of their childhood. Of course, restaurant barbecue—which lacks the open pig, the picnic tables crowded with side dishes, and the dirt under your feet—can never live up to the memory.

Pig roasts were not a part of the culture of my family, my parents being from Texas, where, as any Texan will tell you, barbecue means something altogether different. My sister and I believed special occasions required tacos, the food of my mother's home in the Rio Grande Valley. We always asked for tacos for our birthday dinners and anticipated them every bit as much as we did our birthday cakes. My mother would fry corn tortillas in oil until they blistered and stack them on paper towels to drain. We'd spoon fragrant beef from a napkin-lined bowl into those hot tortillas and fill them with chopped tomatoes and onions, shredded lettuce, and cheese. The cool of the tomatoes against the warm, spicy beef was an undiluted pleasure. And the taste was a taste that was all our family's own. This was the late sixties and early seventies, before fast-food tacos became as ubiquitous as hamburgers. My mother's tacos were as foreign and wondrous to my friends as their families' pig roasts were to me.

Our next-door neighbors, the Rasino family, raised the level of exotic eating in our neighborhood to its most impressive level. Italian Americans who had come to North Carolina via New York City, they made the preparation and sharing of food a way of life. Red tomato gravies that simmered all day, lasagne that Mr. Rasino rose at dawn to assemble, homemade pizza that my friend Jessica loved to eat cold for breakfast, ribbons of crisp dough sprinkled with powdered sugar—the Rasinos seemed never to tire of the kitchen, where so much of the life of the family took place, nor of pressing a visitor to eat more, more. When my father's college students would gather for meals at our house, Mr. Rasino would sometimes prepare a sauce for the spaghetti that they would slurp down in great quantities. He'd stand at our stove, talking with my mother, stirring and tasting, delighted with the challenge of satisfying the enormous appetites of hungry young people. "A person cooking is a person giving," novelist Laurie Colwin writes in *More Home Cooking: A Writer Returns to the Kitchen.* So many of my memories of childhood are of the gifts of cooks.

Eating is "the first and most urgent activity of all animal and human life," the philosopher Leon Kass tells us. "We are only because we eat." But this barely begins to describe what is going on when friends and family put on a pig-pickin', or when a displaced Texan prepares stacks of hot tortillas for her daughters' birthdays, or when an Italian American family gathers around a beautiful lasagne on Christmas day while everyone else on the block dines on the inevitable turkey. We eat to live, it is true. But we also eat to remember where we came from, or to experience a connection with those who first fed us, or to find a place within a new culture, or to celebrate one that has been passed to us from hand to hand, cook by cook. We ask the food we eat to meet many hungers:

the hungers of our body and the hungers of our memory, our hunger for community, and our hunger for home.

The consolation of familiar food for those who are far from home is not, of course, the only use to which we put our food. We often use food as medicine, hoping that particular combinations of fiber and nutrients will ward off disease. And, in fact, food does undeniably affect our health and our moods. Carbohydrates calm us, sugars stimulate us, vitamins and proteins help us heal. Some foods strengthen us; others, consumed regularly, burden us with cholesterol and fat, too much sodium, too many sugars.

Keeping up with which foods are which is a real job: one day chocolate has no redeeming value, the next it is full of protective antioxidants. One day red wine will rot your liver, the next it protects you from cancer. Milk, according to some, provides perfect nutrition; others swear milk consumption will send us to an early grave. Swimming in information, we try to make the best choices we can. We may find ourselves asking, as does memoirist Barbara Grizzuti Harrison in *An Accidental Autobiography,* "Why has eating, an act of animal survival civilized by ritual and refinement, become more complicated than quantum physics?"

Food can play so powerful a role in our lives that we can quickly find ourselves in uneasy relation to it. "I love food," Barbara Harrison writes. "I also see it as the agent of my destruction." The need for food, and even food itself, can be an intolerable burden. The need for food is a burden for those who are hungry and lack the resources to meet that hunger. For those trapped in poverty, the daily struggle for nourishment can be all-consuming, exhausting, and obscenely disheartening in the face of the overabundance of food that our culture presents on every highway, in every mall. Others are burdened by food, not because they don't have enough of it, but because they see it as "an agent of destruction" that will make them fat, and so they spend their days regulating every calorie. Or vomiting up what they do eat. Or not eating at all. Still others are burdened by compulsive overeating that they cannot control.

Is food our friend or our enemy? Is it a gift to be received with thankfulness or a problem to be mastered? It is not surprising that our questions about food are nearly identical to our questions about our bodies. For what other daily activity is more integral to the practice of honoring the body than eating and drinking? How we understand our bodies—as friend or as enemy, as gift or as problem, as sacred or as repulsive, as temple of God's spirit or as a shell in which we are trapped—will influence how and what we eat and drink. How we eat and drink, in turn, helps shape how we feel about our bodies and how those with whom we share our tables feel about theirs.

When we honor our bodies through eating food that both nourishes and delights, we have an opportunity to keep our connections with the earth and with our neighbors visible every day. Our unerasable need to eat and drink confronts us, if we attend to our hunger and our thirst, with the vulnerability of our bodies. And attention to that vulnerability teaches us that we are not self-sufficient but dependent upon God, the earth, and the labor of others. The sustenance we are given in our eating and drinking, if we receive it with gratitude, can teach us to attend to the ways God sustains our lives and draw us into God's work of sustaining all life. The sharing of food can transform our tables into places of refuge where people learn to speak to one another in truth and love. Not for nothing does a shared meal stand at the heart of Christian worship. Not for nothing is the image of the banquet at which all are welcome one of the most persistent images in the Christian tradition of the world to come.

HUNGER AND SATISFACTION

In her beautiful novel *Fasting, Feasting,* Anita Desai describes the moment when Arun, a college student from India spending the summer with a troubled American family, finds the family's daughter, Melanie, lying in her own vomit in the woods. Melanie is bulimic and spends her days bingeing and purging, eating candy bars by the bagful and then vomiting them up. Arun recognizes that he has stumbled onto something quite different from the forced cheerfulness he finds in Melanie's parents: "This is no plastic mock-up, no cartoon representation such as he has been seeing all summer; this is a real pain and a real hunger. But," he wonders, "what hunger does a person so sated feel?"

What kind of hungers *do* sated people feel? I work in a building with a coffee shop downstairs that sells everything from bagels and muffins to pad thai and burritos, along with the usual assortment of chips and candy bars. I am a frequent visitor; I even run a tab. If I don't have time for breakfast at home, I stop in at the coffee shop for a cup of tea and a bagel. At lunch, I'm back for curry and rice and a big bottle of water. And if I have the slightest feeling of hunger in between these meals, especially if I am busy and stressed, I'm back downstairs for a muffin, or a candy bar and a carton of milk. I spend the day sated.

All this food I bring back upstairs to my office, where I eat it while continuing to work. Most of the time I barely notice myself eating and drinking, much less pause to wonder about where the food came from or who rose how early to prepare it. It takes deliberate effort to notice that I am satisfying my hunger with food grown, prepared, and packaged by persons whose names are unknown to me but through whose labor an urgent need of my mine has been satisfied.

There are days, however, as I move up and down the stairs between my office and the coffee shop, when I notice that what I am doing is less like eating and more like fueling. What I do in front of my computer screen with a fork in one hand and an open carton of food in the other has very little to do with what the narratives of the Christian tradition call "breaking bread"—sharing food with others in a way that acknowledges our dependence on our eating for our living, a way of eating together so suffused with gratitude that room is made for honest words to be spoken around the table. What I do alone at my desk is simply to keep hunger at bay, to refuse to feel hunger at all.

Honoring the body through eating and drinking begins with acknowledging the body's hungers. Unless we can experience our body's hungers, we will be cut off from a sense of the vulnerability of our bodies, which need nourishment in order to keep breathing. We will be unable to learn what satisfies us. And we will live unconscious of the ways God sustains our life.

HUNGER AND NEED

Marya Hornbacher, who survived a decade-long embrace of bulimia and anorexia that nearly killed her, writes eloquently in *Wasted: A Memoir of Anorexia and Bulimia* of the cost of refusing to feel or acknowledge one's hungers. An eating disorder, she says, is a "wish to prove that you need nothing, that you have no human hungers, which turns on itself and becomes a searing need for the hunger itself." And, indeed, to stop and consider how dependent we are on food, how quickly the need for food can become all-encompassing, is to know ourselves to be incredibly, even frighteningly vulnerable. As sated with food and drink as many of us are in this culture, though, there are few opportunities to confront this human truth, unless we happen to skip a meal through sheer busyness. And if we do grow hungry during the course of our day, we say (or at least I notice myself saying), "I'm *starving.*" What right does a well-fed American have to reach for such hyperbole? None. But the fact that we do reach for it shows that knowledge of the depth of our need for food is indeed present to us, however unconsciously.

We can become disordered in our eating, Hornbacher suggests, when we do not understand our hungers well enough to respond to them. "At school," she writes, "we were hungry and lost and scared and young and we needed religion, salvation, something to fill the anxious hollow in our chests. Many of us sought it in food and in thinness." Such anxious hollowness is not limited, of course, to young people hungry for meaning. Many of us are unsure of our hungers, how we might feel them, how we might satisfy them. Hornbacher writes, "We know we need and so we acquire and acquire and eat and eat, past the point of bodily fullness, trying to sate a greater need. Ashamed of this, we turn skeletons into goddesses and look to them as if they might teach us how to not-need."

How to "not-need." The attractions are obvious. A person with no hungers, no needs to fulfill, would be immune to pain—powerful. But none of us, no matter how thin or how full we become, is powerful in that way. Not needing to eat quickly undermines our power by becoming not needing to live. And no matter how delicious and filling the meal, the need for the next one is never obliterated. We will be hungry again.

The need for food is that rare thing: a universal fact

of human life, something we all share. But there is enormous variety in how (and whether) our hungers are felt and met. For some, hunger is a daily, minute-by-minute reality. The fact that this is so, in a world in which others are constantly sated, a world in which wars stand between human beings and rudimentary nourishment, is sinful. There is no other way to say it. It is a sign of our distance from God's intentions for creation, for life. If part of the practice of honoring the body involves acknowledging the body's hungers, it also involves working for a world in which the hunger of every human being is met with nourishment. But if we cannot feel our own hungers, how can we learn to imagine and care about the hungers of others?

Because food and drink are so necessary for life and because what we eat and drink suggests so much about who we *are,* faithful practitioners of the world's religions have often thought deeply about how best to order their eating and their drinking. Many faiths have developed forms of preparing and serving, receiving and sharing food and drink as a way of sustaining their relationship with God and one another in the most ordinary of activities. Many religious people have developed ways of renouncing food and drink for a time, thereby heightening attention to the hunger of others, to God's sustaining presence, and to the relationship between hunger for food and hunger for God. Many begin and end their meals with words of blessing and thanksgiving that gather up their gratitude for the sustenance they receive through their eating. These ways of eating and drinking often crystallize in a ritual form in which the same food and the same words are shared each time, like the Passover seder, or the Lord's Supper. But religious ways of eating and drinking have implications not only for how we worship but also for how we eat and drink from day to day.

MANNA RHYTHMS

Throughout the Hebrew Bible and the New Testament, story after story is told of God responding to human hunger with compassion. One story that is particularly suggestive for developing a way of life that honors the body is the story of God's providing food for the people of Israel as they traveled through the desert after their escape from slavery in Egypt. Hungry and tired and deep into the wilderness, the people turned to Moses to complain; We'd rather be slaves in Egypt, they said, where at least we were provided with meat and bread, than starve to death out here.

God responds to these complaints by promising to provide meat in the evenings and bread every morning. Every evening the camp fills with quails, and in the morning, a fine, flaky food tasting of wafers made with honey lies all over the ground, just beneath the dew. It is this mysterious food that occasions the most discussion in Exodus 16; the quails, being more familiar, come and go without much comment.

The people of Israel call this wafery food *manna,* which means "what is it?" And indeed manna had properties that were difficult to explain. Even when some people gathered more and others gathered less, in the end, everyone had the right amount, just enough for the day. God warned them not to hoard it, to trust that it would appear new every morning. Whenever anyone tried to save some for the next day, it rotted and filled with worms. The one exception to this was the sixth day, when each person could gather enough for two days in order to observe a sabbath day of rest on the seventh. The extra food did not spoil and so the people of Israel could rest from the work of gathering food for one day. Some industrious folk headed out on the seventh day to gather more manna and found none. God wants you to *rest,* Moses said to them. You have enough food for today. Go home and rest.

The story of Israel being sustained by manna in the desert is a story of God honoring the bodies of God's beloved people and teaching them, over the course of forty years, a way of life that would sustain them from one generation to the next. This way of life was, and is, marked by gratitude and trust—gratitude for God's gifts, new every morning, and trust that God would continue to provide from day to day. The people were taught not to hoard, in fear of the future, but to gather what they needed for one day only—just as, later, Jesus would teach his disciples to pray for enough bread for "this day." Israel was taught to live within a rhythm of six days of work and one of rest, a rhythm that allowed them to flourish. And they were taught to see God's presence in

HONORING THE BODY

the sustenance God provided: when you wake in the morning to find manna resting on the ground, "then you shall know that I am the Lord your God."

The habit of trust that God sought to instill in Israel is perhaps the most difficult to learn today. Remember Y2K? We were urged to stockpile bottled water and canned goods in case the world's computers crashed. Prominent fundamentalist ministers were among the most urgent of the voices of alarm. Private militias and "survivalists"—many of whom claim the name Christian—make hoarding an obsession every year, not just at the turn of the millennium. They take the shape of their life not from Israel's experience in the desert but from doomsday scenarios in which only their careful accumulation of food and weapons allows them to survive the approaching calamity.

It's easy to criticize extremists. But what if all the world's computers *had* crashed on January 1, 2000? I certainly don't claim to have been immune to worry about Y2K. The only reason I didn't have a pantry full of canned beans and bottled water is that I'm not well enough organized. What does it mean to trust God in a world in which we have set systems in place that might, in fact, one day fail us? What does it mean to trust God when our unbalanced distribution of resources means that some people have easy access to food while others do not?

It's easy to "trust in God" when our grocery stores are full to overflowing, when we have the means to pick and choose what we'd like to eat each day. But what if one is not accustomed to the overabundance of Western supermarkets? What if one has to hoard what little one has in order to feed one's family? What if experience has taught not the manna-lessons of Israel but the hunger-lessons of deprivation? A mother who adopted a child from an orphanage reports that months after bringing the child into her home, months after offering meal after healthful meal, she still finds little stashes of food in her child's room—a crust of bread in a sock drawer, a pile of mashed potatoes in the closet. It may be years before her daughter can trust that the abundance of her new home will last. This may take as many years as it took for her to learn that she could not depend on others to nourish her, that she could not expect to receive enough to eat each day to ease her gnawing hunger.

In a world where children learn such terrible lessons, can we call God trustworthy, much less trust that God will provide? Can we trust that God established creation in such a way that all life can be nourished, that no one need go hungry? Can we trust God the way that the author of Psalm 104 trusts God? In the midst of a hymn of praise to the God who stretched out the sky, set the earth on its foundations, and created life in abundant, extravagant variety comes a few verses of thanksgiving to God as the feeder of hungers, the trustworthy nourisher of life.

> These all look to you to give them their food in due
>   season;
> when you give it to them, they gather it up;
> when you open your hand, they are filled with good
> things [Psalm 104:27–28].

God made the earth to support life, the psalmist sings. The turning of the seasons, the sun, the wind, and the rain all work together for God's purpose of giving life, nourishing life, sustaining life. How wondrously it all works; how good to live within creation's rhythms of exertion and rest, planting and gathering, receiving and giving, life and death.

I believe that we can trust God to provide because God *has* provided. God has provided the garden of this world. God continues, moment by moment, breath by breath, to sustain life itself.

There is enough here for all. But all do not have enough, not nearly enough. It is not God who needs to be overcome in order that all may eat. It is human greed, human grasping, human violence that must be overcome. It is human sin, in which we all have a share.

What would manna look like in our own day? It would look like food generously shared from hand to hand. It would look like communities that take responsibility for the well-being and nourishment of others. It would look like a world that attends to and feels human hunger and which responds by learning to eat in ways that allow all to have their hunger met.

That is why table blessings so often hold together gratitude for God's sustenance and remembrance of those who hunger. For remembering the one should lead us to think of the other. Every time we sit down to a meal, we should remember two things: that life is sustained by God and that there are many, beloved by God, who do not have enough to eat. Gratitude and solidarity, practiced over and over, three times each day, ought to shape not only how we receive our nourishment but how we receive our neighbor as well. As the author of the

Nourishing the Body

letter of James puts it, "If a brother or sister is naked and lacks daily food, and one of you says to them, 'Go in peace; keep warm and eat your fill,' and yet you do not supply their bodily needs, what is the good of that?" (James 3:16).

The rhythm of life that the people of Israel learned through living off manna in the wilderness was a rhythm of work and rest, trust and gratitude. It was a life-giving rhythm undergirded by God's intention that everyone have enough. This rhythm of eating requires no calorie counting and discourages eating far past the point of fullness. It is a rhythm that works against hurried lunches gulped down at one's desk. It is a rhythm that can ease our anxiety about food as an enemy and loosen our dependence on food as a drug. It is a rhythm that teaches us to eat with others in mind. If we could figure out how to live within manna rhythms in a world so conflicted about food, we might find ourselves liberated to feel and meet our hungers in ways that are good not only for ourselves but also for the communities and the world in which we live.

KEEPING KOSHER

Stories of God satisfying human hunger persist throughout the stories of Israel. Some of the best are the stories of Elijah, whom God keeps well nourished, sending ravens to bring him food, replenishing the meager bread and oil of a widow who offers him hospitality. When Elijah is being chased by the assassins of Queen Jezebel, he is met by an angel who brings him food. Like my neighbors, the Rasinos, who could never be convinced that one had eaten enough, the angel keeps waking Elijah to say, Get up and eat. You'll never survive your journey if you don't eat.

But the story of Israel is not just the story of miraculous meals of angel food. It is also the story of the ordering of daily eating and drinking, of placing food and its preparation at the heart of the life of faith. The ancient rules about food preparation and consumption codified in the Hebrew Bible and interpreted by the rabbis give shape and flavor to holiness, inviting those who adhere to them to contemplate, as anthropologist Mary Douglas puts it, "the oneness, purity and completeness of God . . . in every encounter with the animal kingdom and at every meal." These rules, observed through the centuries and in our own day, continue to shape the consciousness and pattern the days of the individuals, families, and communities that observe them, to nurture in them respect for life and attention to the history of which they are a part.

I read a book recently about one year in the life of a woman who, cautiously, but with no small yearning, began to embrace the Jewish laws of *kashrut*. Jewish by birth, culture, and inclination, the author, Elizabeth Ehrlich, had nevertheless not been raised in a wholly observant household. After she marries and has children, however, she begins to spend time in her mother-in-law's kitchen. Her mother-in-law, Miriam, takes the shape of every day from Jewish observance, keeping alive not only ancient religious practices but also recipes from a Polish community destroyed by the Nazis, recipes that would otherwise be lost. Ehrlich begins to be drawn to Miriam's ways of sanctifying the everyday work of preparing food. And so she begins to take her first steps toward keeping kosher. "I took my little step," she writes, "and, eventually, the world quivered."

What happened when this young working mother who wasn't even sure she believed in God began to separate dishes to be used for meat from dishes to be used for dairy, when she began to prepare days in advance in order to greet the sabbath with a clean house and delicious food on the table, when she gave herself over to arduous Passover preparations? Well, for one thing, she worried. She worried about emphasizing difference and separation in a world already so divided. She worried about being caught in a lifestyle that keeps the mother always cooking and cleaning. She worried about how to teach her children to embrace *kashrut* without scorning the food that others eat. She wondered if the kosher laws could possibly still be "rules to live by, for those such as me, raised to pick and choose, raised without God."

But as each month found her closer to a kosher life, as she gave up shellfish and feeding her children from fast-food outlets, her life, and the life of her family, changed and deepened. They began eating together, at home, more often than not. They ate with gratitude. They felt connected, through their eating, with those who had gone before them, those who had kept the traditions alive even when they may have wished to do otherwise. They felt themselves taking responsibility for those traditions. They began to feel it was their turn.

Ehrlich also found in the prohibitions against eating meat with blood in it, and against eating meat with milk, an honest reckoning with human hunger and human appetite: "If you are going to slaughter an animal for food, respect it. Never forget that it lived and breathed, a mammal like yourself. Here is a way of reminding, respecting—eat the animal separate from the milk. Thus the tradition comes to terms with human appetite, but demands consciousness."

Eating according to kosher laws means eating with awareness: awareness of hunger, of appetite, of life mysteriously sustained. It means taking time with decisions about what to eat and how to prepare it; it means *eating*, not fueling.

But Ehrlich is quick to insist that "you don't keep kosher for heightened awareness." You keep kosher because it's in the Torah. You keep kosher because it's a commandment of God. And through her attempt to embrace that commandment, she found a way of living that finds in hunger and the satisfying of hunger God's movement in history and deepens the significance of the ordinary tasks of setting the table and cleaning up: "You are only washing your dishes, but you are doing something more. You are tending something ancient, and it matters. That meat knife matters. Your work matters."

As the months turn and Ehrlich and her family

commit themselves more and more to an observant, kosher life, she finds that her doubts about God's existence are not erased but, rather, are set inside a different context. She finds that her doubts and her intermittent sense of eternity touching the everyday in the practices she has taken on can live together: "Not that I believe in a world to come. But a roasted chicken on Friday night after candles are lit and lights are turned low and blessings are said, in a clean house, is for the moment, paradise enough."

I loved Ehrlich's book. I bought it at a conference in Boston, began reading it while standing in line to check in at the airport, read it all the way home, and didn't stop reading it until I was finished. Like all the best books, it made me imagine my life in new ways. It made me dream of more regular mealtimes for my family, more deliberately chosen food. It made me want to recover my own family's traditions—those tacos!—and pass them on to my daughter. It made me long to abandon my rushed, unmindful lunches at the computer, to find in the daily preparation and eating of food a way to remember the holy.

What might this mean for a Christian? In our culture, the Christian embrace of liberty in eating has had the effect of allowing us to live as if anything can be eaten, as if boundaries and limits are only for others. A Christian writer, Garret Keizer, worried recently that Christian liberty in eating has become a way of affirming "if it tastes good, eat it," a "commandment," he says, upon which hang "all the law and the profits."

Keizer wonders if it might be possible for Christians to eat in a kosher way. He wonders what would happen if Christians adopted "two or three dietary restrictions prayerfully chosen, freely embraced and widely observed." The refusal he advocates is the purchase and consumption of factory-produced chicken. He believes we should refuse to support this method of producing large quantities of poultry because it undermines family farmers, damages the health of poultry workers, and introduces unwanted chemicals into the bodies of those who eat it. He believes Christians should care about these things and make choices that reflect our faith in a God who desires the good of all.

A way of eating that draws deeply on Christian faith would be shaped by such choices, choices that honor the body—our bodies and the bodies of others. Choices that delight in the bounty of creation and respect God's intention that there be enough for all. Some choices that would make a difference in my own life and would make me more mindful that food is God's gift to us are ones like these: fasting from fast food. Eating less meat. Paying attention to my body's hunger and then eating no more than I need to satisfy it. Taking care never to let food go to waste (a perennial problem in my refrigerator). Really trying to eat those five fruits and vegetables every day that our bodies need to thrive. Never eating without giving thanks. Even a few such choices, embraced with consciousness, might teach us what Elizabeth Ehrlich has learned, that in the midst of the ordinary activities of preparing and eating food we might touch something holy and find our lives changed. And our bodies might become for us not only a sign of our mortality and vulnerability but also the place where we meet God.

Chapter 6

BLESSING OUR TABLE LIFE

———

Since reading Elizabeth Ehrlich's book, I have tried to take more care with our family's evening meal. Just the other night, my husband and daughter carefully set the table, I cooked a more balanced than usual meal, we lit candles, and we all sat down to sing a blessing.

Now that I have a three-year-old, I know where the tradition of holding hands for the blessing comes from— from parents trying to keep their children's hands out of the food while grace is being said.

Throughout the meal, our daughter would take a bite of food, and then hop down from her chair, wander away, and drift back for another bite. "Sit *down,*" we said. "Let's enjoy a good meal together, let's talk." "Okay," she said as she fidgeted herself out of her chair for the fifth time, her vegetables untouched. "Can I have my dessert now?"

Imagine my relief when I read this in Laurie Colwin's *More Home Cooking:* "It is my opinion that Norman Rockwell and his ilk have done more to make already anxious people feel more guilty than anyone else. I myself am reduced to worm size when contemplating his famous illustration of the farm family Thanksgiving table, with the beaming grandparents and the children with their hair combed. How happy they all look! And how politely and still the children sit! Why can't I get my child to sit like that? And when her cousins come to a family dinner, why do they all *wander* so much?"

Well, thank God, I thought, it's not just *my* family.

I'm not going to give up on family meals, shared together, seasoned with good conversation, however. I believe that all people need to be undergirded by what Colwin calls "table life," particularly young growing people. They need a table life in which good food is obviously enjoyed in order to withstand the pressures of a culture that tells them that dangerously thin bodies are more beautiful than other bodies. They need a table life in which delight is taken in food in all its variety to resist those who tell them that they would excel in the sport they love if they would only lose weight or gain weight or bulk up on protein alone. They need a table life in which everyone's voice is of equal importance, and they need to be fed not only on healthful food but also on delicious words of gratitude. They need to learn what it means to offer hospitality, to keep a space open at the table for the unexpected guest. They need the experience that a lively table life can offer, of seeing others as they really are and of being known, really known, in their own right.

Such a rich and vigorous table life has to be taught, and getting good at it takes some practice. We are certainly not born with the basic skills that are required: sitting in your seat, waiting to eat until all have been served and the blessing said or sung, learning to handle a knife and fork, listening to others, entering a conversation, learning what and how much will satisfy your hunger. All of these abilities have to be learned, cultivated meal by meal.

WORDS

The words that are shared around the table are vital to the life shared there. The table life of Christians and Jews begins, and sometimes ends, with words of gratitude, words that not only offer thanks to God for our food but also open a space for other words to be spoken with care. My family has experimented with different blessings to open our meals. Sometimes my daughter, who attends a Jewish preschool, blesses the meal in Hebrew words her father and I don't understand, but in which we can hear the thanksgiving of centuries. Sometimes we sing a blessing to the tune of "Doxology."

> Be present at our table, Lord.
> Be here and everywhere adored.
> These mercies bless and grant that we
> May strengthened for thy service be.

Sometimes we read the passage from Psalm 104 about all creatures, and us among them, looking to God to give us our food in due season: "When you give it to them, they gather it up; when you open your hand, they are filled with good things" (Psalm 104:28).

I have two minister friends who, when they sit down for supper at the end of the day, sometimes feel all prayed out. And so they have adopted a silent Quaker blessing to begin their meals. When our family is privileged to join them for supper, I always love that blessing. Hand in hand, eyes closed, I can feel the worries of the day gathered up in that silence, to be replaced, at least for a time, by an awareness of how fortunate we are to have good food, family, and friends to join hands with. The first words spoken out of that silence, even if they are "please help yourself to the string beans," are always precious.

Laurie Colwin remembers that in her childhood, you did not join the table life of the family until you were able "to take part in dinner-time conversation (which in those days was considered an art form)." When meals are eaten on the run or with the television on, we risk losing that art form. When we avoid difficult topics, when we talk our way around our worries and questions, we risk losing that art form. Even those who eat alone can make meals a time of reflection on things that truly matter.

Table life, as we all know, can have its shadow side. If you grew up in a family in which one parent stayed home all day with children while the other parent went off to work, you may remember your family's table life as a collision of worlds, marked by irritability. And certainly we all know what it's like to reach the end of a day frazzled and worn. We all know what it's like to want to sit down to a quiet meal, only to have a partner or a child or a friend want more from us than we have to give. Cultivating a rich table life is not all Norman Rockwell–style coziness. It takes a lot of work.

I came to consciousness of my own family's table life in the late years of the Vietnam War. We shared news at suppertime, and often that news was of the war. We talked about the war, and that talk was often anguished. We talked about politics and candidates and elections. And guests at our table—such as the monk who had walked from North Carolina to Washington, D.C. to protest the war, or students whose faith had been challenged by the war—made the conversation even more fervent. When my grandparents joined us at our table, that talk often became more of a debate, and I learned how people who love each other hold conversations on painful subjects about which they deeply disagree. And I learned that even in the midst of profound disagreement, food could still be shared.

It is our bodies that make such sharing possible. It is the vulnerability of our bodies—our *need* for food—that sends us back to the table, even sometimes in spite of ourselves. So often our bodily vulnerability seems like a constraint, a limit. But in the context of eating and drinking, of gathering with others for a meal because we must eat to live, what has seemed to limit us actually *opens* us—not only to the food our bodies need but also to relationships with those with whom we share food. Through the needs of our bodies, God opens us to one another. Every time we gather for meals with others, God offers us an opportunity to go deeper in our conversations, to plumb our disagreements, to change one another, to forge new bonds. It is our bodies—hungry, thirsty, needy—that bring us to a place where this is possible.

Some people have a natural gift for conversation around the table. They have interesting things to say, and they know how to elicit interesting things from others, even the most shy. I have to admit that I am not one of those people. At the end of a day, I have a tendency to stare off into space as I eat. Not that a little silence in a meal is an unwelcome thing. Indeed it is not. But conversation over food is about staying connected with those with whom we break bread, and about making room for others to say what is important to them and offering our own thoughts. Such conversation cannot be had without taking some risks—choosing to speak of what is in our hearts and inviting those with whom we eat to speak of what is in theirs, rather than filling the silence with empty chatter. But good conversation is a wonder that cannot be stage managed. A good conversation over a meal just takes off, and we are left afterwards to marvel at it, at how it fed us every bit as much as the food did.

Some people not only begin their meals with a blessing but end them with a blessing as well. My family didn't say any formal blessing at the end of our meals when I was a child, but my father would often lean back in his chair before we all got up from the table, take a deep breath, and exhale the word "Ephphatha." *Ephphatha* is an Aramaic word that Mark's Gospel records Jesus saying as he unstopped the ears of a man who could not hear. It means "be opened." But my dad didn't say it because of what it meant. He said it because he liked the way it *sounded*. It was a word he could sigh out, after a delicious meal, in complete satisfaction. So when I come across *ephphatha* in the Bible, I have to remember that it means "be opened." Because for me it means *Thank you*. It means *I have eaten and am satisfied*. It means *I am so glad to be around this table with these people*.

Perhaps, though, my father's sigh of satisfaction did refer to the literal meaning of *ephphatha*. Rather than a command to be open, perhaps it became, in my father's use of it, an acknowledgment that he had *been* opened by this meal, that he had been opened to something greater than himself in the simple bodily act of sharing food with those he loves. Once again, it is our bodies, so often associated with mortality and limits, that open us to transcendence. Our bodies need not be like stoppers in a man's ears that block his access to God and others. Some meals open us up. And our bodies lead the way there.

FOOD

Everyone has to learn to eat. Contrary to what we think about breastfeeding being "natural," even babies and mothers have to learn how to do it. Little children at the table need to learn also. If she had her way, my daughter would live on bread alone. I have to help her learn to love carrots and pears and strawberries and broccoli, too.

Anne Lamott writes in *Traveling Mercies* of learning to eat as a thirty-three-year-old woman. Caught in a cycle of bingeing and purging, frightened at the damage it was doing to her body, she sought help. She was lucky to find a counselor who taught her that what she needed to learn to do was to feel her hunger and respond to it with care. She was lucky to find someone who told her that she would overcome her illness if she would cherish her body. "It is, finally, so wonderful," she writes, "to have learned how to eat, to taste and love what slips down my throat, padding me, filling me up, that I'm not uncomfortable calling it a small miracle."

A rich table life, rooted in gratitude, can teach us a way of eating that honors the needs and appetites of our bodies. In our culture, we live in the midst of such plenty, where "special occasion" food is available every day, in every store and every restaurant, that it is easy to forget how to pattern our eating according to ordinary days and days dedicated to feasting or fasting. We could feast every night if we had enough money. But does the fact that we can mean that we should?

Feasting every day dulls our appetite and diminishes the occasions that cry out for a feast. But the rhythm of eating suggested by the manna story—a rhythm of six ordinary days and one feast day—helps us savor our food and deepens our celebrations. Eating regular, simple meals all week makes that Friday night roast chicken on a table adorned with candles a paradise for Elizabeth Ehrlich. Because we did not have them every night, my mother's tacos made our birthdays and other family feast days especially delicious. A pig roast is so labor intensive that it can only be managed every once in a while and the barbecue is more savory because of it.

Those who try to live according to sacred time—such as Jews who keep the sabbath and Christians who follow the liturgical year—are invited by their traditions into a rhythm of ordinary days punctuated by festivals and fasts. And eating is a way to mark the difference. For Christians, every Sunday is a festival day, and, for many, every Sunday is a day to gather for the shared meal of the church, the Lord's Supper. Abundant Sunday dinners have also been a way in which Christians have welcomed and celebrated the Lord's Day. Or Saturday night dinners big enough so that there are delicious leftovers to eat on Sunday, and the cooks can have a rest.

The weekly rhythm of ordinary days and one festival day is magnified in the large celebrations of the Christian church—Christmas, which follows the dark introspection of Advent, and Easter, which follows the Lenten fast. We experience these feasts fully only by preparing for them through the quieter weeks that precede them, weeks that invite us to let our hunger build through eating plainer food.

Eating within a rhythm of ordinary days and feast days can sharpen our attention to the gift of food and teach us to delight in the smell and texture and taste of it. And we will learn to know our appetite and our

Blessing Our Table Life

hunger; we will learn how to know what we need, what will satisfy.

My mother used to tell me that my eyes were bigger than my stomach. In other words, I would put more food on my plate than I could actually eat. I still have this problem. I always seem, for example, to cook way more spaghetti than my family can eat in one sitting. And so I put the rest in a plastic container, only to remember it the next week, when it is no longer edible. In the home of my mother's childhood, food was carefully prepared and consumed. Nothing was wasted. They were frugal because they had to be frugal. My mother is baffled and offended by wasted food.

Elizabeth Ehrlich writes of Miriam's insistence on the stewardship of food in her kitchen. Miriam wastes nothing—every gesture has its purpose, every spoon its use, and every morsel of food goes to nourishing the bodies of her family. Miriam's father had starved to death in Buchenwald. Food is not wasted in Miriam's kitchen.

This is an important part of learning to eat: learning to steward food, learning to buy and prepare and consume what you need without letting any go to waste. I find that this takes real planning. My husband is good at it: he pays attention to how much we are eating and drinking and goes to the grocery store knowing exactly how much milk and juice and cereal and spaghetti we'll need for a week. On those rare occasions when I do the shopping, I make a list, but then so much else looks good to me once I get to the store. It's a real discipline to shop for food. It's a discipline to know how much to bring

HONORING THE BODY

home, how much to prepare, and even, how much to eat. It's a discipline to know how much is enough. But it's a discipline that makes us attentive to our hunger and our appetite and helps us live in the consciousness of the hunger and needs of others.

HOSPITALITY

In his memoirs, the Nobel prize–winning novelist Elias Canetti remembers the Passover seders of his childhood in Bulgaria: the thorough cleaning of the house, the brown eggs boiled in coffee, the long table with room for many, many guests. "The whole family gathered for the seder, which was celebrated in our home. It was customary to pull in two or three strangers off the street; they were seated at the feast and participated in everything."

What a fortunate boy he was to have grown up with a table life rich enough and well established enough for there to be room for complete strangers to join in. Is it any wonder that the boy grew up to be a writer in whose works concern for human flourishing haunts every page?

We are lucky indeed when the life around our table is spacious enough for those outside our household to be included. When we invite others, especially others in need of what our table has to offer—to be seated and served, nourished and listened to—our tables become holy places, a sign of what God desires. "When you give a banquet," Jesus says in Luke 14, "invite the poor, the crippled, the lame, and the blind." In Jesus' teachings, earthly banquets at which the poor are included and given seats of honor reflect the table life of God.

Christian table life must always have room for unexpected guests. It can never be a closed system to which only the familiar and acceptable are welcome. I believe this to be true of the table life in Christian homes. I believe it also to be true of the table life of Christian churches—above all, at the Lord's Supper. Nearly every time we see Jesus eating in the Gospels, we see him sitting down with those who are, in one way or another, unacceptable. Jesus' own table life had room for all, an openness we are called to imitate.

A vibrant table life can teach such hospitality. And only a vibrant table life can risk such hospitality. We learn first in small ways: to pass the food around the table, to share the food that is there, to eat portions that allow all at the table to be filled. We learn to share food and conversation with those with whom we live. We learn to include others in our meal through prayers spoken over the food, prayers that gather up the needs of the world.

How do we get from there to inviting strangers off the street to our tables? Different people forge different paths. I have a friend who lives alone, who worries that it would not be safe to invite a stranger to her table. But she has no problem inviting a hungry person she meets on the street to join her for a meal at a restaurant and does so regularly.

My friend Anna Lee, raised with the lively table life of an extended Korean American family, found herself drawn to the feeding ministry of the parish where she worked and worshiped. She brought her stories of this ministry to her family's table. And now her whole family spends each Thanksgiving Day at the soup kitchen, preparing, serving, and sharing a festive meal—and the good conversation that makes a feast a feast—with others.

I know a family that so delights in their life together that they feel a particular responsibility to share meals with those who are lonely for good company. This family prepares a big pot of soup on Saturday night in order to be prepared to bring someone home from church for lunch the next day—someone who has lost a beloved companion, someone recently divorced, someone who lives alone. This practice has made them particularly attentive to their community, to the tender, painful places in the lives of others. And they find that they receive as much as they give at their shared Sunday meals.

When we attempt to offer hospitality to others, we learn again about the integrity and relationality of our bodies. For though our bodies are separate, it is through our bodies that we enter into relationship with others: joining hands in blessing, passing a plate of food. The needs of the body, the hungers of the body, can certainly lead to a closed table life that seeks only to satisfy the self. But the needs of the body can also open a wide and spacious path to community in which bread that is blessed, broken, and shared becomes the food of angels.

Seeing Ourselves and Others as We Really Are

A table life in which we are taught to savor and share our food, to speak and receive honest words, and to welcome others with care and reverence is a table life in which we might learn to see others as they really are and in which we ourselves might be deeply known.

In a story about Jesus in the days after his Resurrection, we find two of Jesus' disciples walking to the village of Emmaus, talking of Jesus' death. Jesus himself joins them on the road, but they do not recognize him. They are captivated by his conversation and invite him to stay the evening with them. When they sit down to eat, he blesses and breaks the bread, and they recognize him at last. It is the sharing of food that makes it possible for the disciples to see, really see, who is with them (Luke 24).

I have learned about the way a meal—and in particular the meal of the Lord's Supper—can help us see ourselves and others as we really are from my friend Diana Ventura. Diana is in the midst of seminary education, learning to be the minister God is calling her to be. She is smart and funny and an exceptionally good listener, and so she has done very well. But she began to get a little tense, a little nervous, before her field education, her year of supervised ministry in a parish, began. She finally admitted that what she was anxious about was her role as cupbearer during the Eucharist, a task her teaching pastor had asked her to assume. Having been born with cerebral palsy, Diana jerks a bit when she walks and drags one leg. She was afraid, *really* afraid, that she would spill the cup on the floor or, worse, on someone she was serving. But, being Diana, she didn't ask to be relieved of this duty; she gave it a try. And things went well. Nothing spilled, but she remained extremely vigilant.

One spring Sunday, Diana served again as cup-bearer and walked from person to person kneeling at the rail at the front of her church, offering them a drink. "The blood of Christ," she said to each one, "the cup of salvation." And as she raised the cup to each person's lips, taking the utmost care not to fall, she saw her own reflection in the shiny silver chalice. Over and over again, she saw the reflection of her body in the cup. *This is my broken body,* she thought, *serving this church. This is my body, teaching people what we do with brokenness in the church. Here in this cup is new life, and here is my body, expressing the truth of what this new life means!*

In the table life of God, we are received and welcomed, our bodies blessed and nourished. In the table life of God, we are seen as we really are, and we are deeply known. In the table life of God, nothing is wasted, not even our own brokenness.

Blessing Our Table Life

Chapter 7

EXERTING AND RESTING THE BODY

———

I've been noticing, as I watch my daughter and her schoolmates fearlessly climbing and swinging on the playground, dancing and running with unselfconscious joy, how much pleasure children take in the exertion of their bodies and the testing of their bodies' capacities. Parents may be reminded of the body's vulnerability as we watch children dangle upside down from the highest rung on the monkey bars, but they, clearly, revel in the body's reach and strength.

Some people are lucky enough to hold onto that feeling their whole lives. My friend Diana, partially disabled by cerebral palsy, inhabits her body with such vigor that it's possible to glimpse the little girl she once was, playing basketball ferociously with her brothers, mastering ice skating with determination. My husband is another one: hardly a daylight hour passed in his childhood that he didn't have a street hockey stick or a basketball in his hands. And even now, as a forty-year-old divinity school professor, he still walks, as one of our friends puts it, like he's looking for the basket.

I remember childhood joy in bodily exertion— especially in swimming and dancing. I remember also the dilution of that joy and its gradual replacement with self-consciousness about my body and reluctance to exert myself—at least in the presence of others.

When I was a child, my dad and I played a lot of catch. He gave me a beautiful mitt, taught me how to pitch a fastball and a curveball. In the green sanctuary of our backyard, I felt I could do anything. But at school I was awkward and clumsy and couldn't catch a big rubber kickball, much less a baseball. I was also a slow runner, always coming in last. So, naturally, I was assigned to a footrace during our seventh-grade field day. I confided my fears about this race to my mother, who loved to run. She began running before the running craze began, first around our backyard, and then around our neighborhood, in white thin-soled Keds (this was also before the running shoe craze began). "Wear my sneakers!" she said. "They are soft and light, and you'll feel like you're running on air."

So I did. I wore her white Keds with the soft thin soles. And she was right: I felt as light as a whisper, fast and strong. I flew toward the finish line thinking, "So *this* is what it feels like to run *fast!*" But when I crossed it, I was greeted with wild laughter and shouts of "Windmill!" Evidently what I had experienced as speed and strength had looked, instead, like a girl careening down her lane with her arms flailing. The name "Windmill" followed me for years, and I began to take care never to be seen running. I began to slow down.

It was a long time before I again felt the joy I had felt running in my mother's shoes. But in graduate school I fell in love with a man who ran with effortless grace, who took pleasure both in the steady rhythms of a long run and the lung-expanding, leg-pounding exhilaration of a sprint. He was (and still is) beautiful to watch as he ran. As we sat for long hours in the library, writing papers, studying for exams, he would sometimes say to me, "Let's go out for a run together. We need to clear our minds, shake off some stress." And I'd demur, "No, I don't run, don't know how, really. Let's go for a long walk instead." Mostly he said, "Okay," and walked with me, but finally, one night, he said, "No, let's go to the gym and run, it'll feel so good." I was in love, so I said, "Well, sure, why not?"

He suggested we start out slowly, running a mile and a half, twelve laps around the track. I had never run a mile and a half in my life, but okay, we started running. Within two laps, my lungs were burning. But within four, I was starting to feel my stride lengthen as we ran side by side; I started to feel myself speeding up. By the time we began closing in on our twelfth lap, I was panting and groaning loudly enough for everyone on the track to hear, but Kevin kept saying, "You're doing great, let's finish big, let's speed up at the end." And in a burst of energy, I did. I sprinted down the last half of the track,

Exerting and Resting the Body

Kevin matching me stride for stride, and felt in every muscle the pleasure of exertion, of pushing my body beyond its boundaries. It was a physical pleasure, the pleasure of feeling myself wholly embodied, of feeling blood and breath moving through me. It was a spiritual pleasure, the relief of feeling old fears and inhibitions drained of their power, a feeling of freedom and possibility. And it was a sexual pleasure, the pleasure of feeling someone I love drawing out my strength, urging me on, matching his body's rhythm to mine. It is one of my husband's enduring gifts to me that he reintroduced me to the joy of bodily exertion. Through honoring my body and its strength, he helped me begin to do the same.

The other thing I felt as I ran around the track that day was the regret of wasted time. I wished I'd not cared so much about being teased about my body's excesses. I wished I'd kept right on running in those white Keds. I wished I'd been smart enough to join my mother on her evening runs around the neighborhood, wished I'd let her help me develop speed and endurance. I wished I'd let my joy in the movement of my body govern my decisions about when and how I'd exert myself, wished I'd tested my body's limits, wished I'd been less self-conscious. But, of course, it's easy to imagine feeling brave in the face of childhood teasing with the hindsight of an adult, and much more difficult when one is a child. I remember that as I watch my daughter and her friends in their uninhibited play and wish them a joy in their embodiment so deeply planted that nothing can diminish it.

Fearfully and Wonderfully Made

The authors of scripture are forever holding up a mirror to our bodies, trying to make us see the imprint of the divine on our unruly flesh. "So God created humankind in his image," the author of Genesis writes, "in the image of God he created them" (Genesis 1:27). "I praise you," sings the psalmist, "for I am fearfully and wonderfully made" (Psalm 139:14). "Do you not know," Paul asks, incredulous, "that your body is a temple of the Holy Spirit?" (I Corinthians 6:19).

But how many of us, when we gaze into the mirror, see God's image reflected back at us? Most of us see instead things about our bodies we'd like to change. Some of us see bellies that refuse to lie flat. Others worry over bottoms that spread too far or muscles we wish were more defined. Even the most trim and fit among us find things to criticize: legs too short or shoulders too small, imperfect posture or inadequate height. It is the rare person who is moved to praise by the scrutiny of his or her own body.

The bodies of others, however, do sometimes evoke our praise and wonderment. And often they do this through feats of bodily exertion. Think of Michael Jordan flying toward the basket, ball controlled by one outstretched hand, all his muscles taut. Think of Olympic runners and swimmers, gymnasts and skaters, beautiful in their strength and speed. Writing of Red Barber, the great radio announcer for the Brooklyn Dodgers,

Exerting and Resting the Body

Barbara Grizzuti Harrison describes him as "the lyricist of my childhood, a man who instructed me in the beauties of the body—he talked about the muscles and sinews and dance of a baseball player, and I saw the hand of God in His creation more vividly than I saw it at all the Bible studies my mother took me to."

Just as highly trained and disciplined athletes can evoke our sense of wonder at what the human body can do, so the athletes themselves often describe some experience of transcendence that happens when they push their bodies as far as they can. Diane Ackerman considers such descriptions in her book *Deep Play*. She reports that basketball player Patsy Neal describes transcendent moments in the midst of a game as "a state of grace, or an act of faith . . . precious moments of pure ecstasy." Steve McKinney, who set the downhill world record for speed skiing of 124 miles per hour, described his life as a quest for stillness in the midst of movement. "Up in those high couloirs," he explained, "I have my talks with God." The great dancer Isadora Duncan wrote that, when dancing, "the flesh becomes light and transparent, a luminous moving cloud . . . the whole of its divinity." But the ecstasy of the dance is not limited to the dancer alone. Duncan's sister-in-law, Margherita Duncan, remembers that when audiences watched Duncan dance, "we felt as if we had received the blessing of God."

What is it about watching human beings in beautiful motion, human beings pressing against the limits of what the body can do, that makes us feel as if we had received the blessing of God? Why do these bodies moving at the extreme edge of exertion not inspire the kinds of feelings that looking at the thin, exquisitely dressed bodies that our culture everywhere celebrates do—namely, feelings of dissatisfaction with our own bodies and frustration that our bodies do not and most likely cannot look like the bodies of fashion models and movie stars? Shouldn't the athletes' unattainable feats of bodily excellence depress us as well? Why do they instead lift us up?

Perhaps it is because, while a particular body shape and an expensive wardrobe may be out of our reach, testing our strength and endurance is not. I certainly can't play basketball like Patsy Neal or Michael Jordan, but I can test my own limits in a basketball game with friends. I will never know what Steve McKinney once called the "beautiful weird flight" down a glacier, but I might catch a glimpse of the "stillness" he speaks of in a long (albeit slow!) run. I'll never be as graceful as Isadora Duncan, but when my daughter and I put on music and dance our hearts out, we do taste joy. Everyone's limits are different —some press against them from the seats of their wheelchairs, some on the slopes of high mountains, some in the streets and parks of their neighborhood. The history of the body is in part the history of its own striving to surpass itself. "Human beings are their bodies," writes Dartmouth religion professor Amy Hollywood, "and yet bodies themselves continually push toward transcendence of bodily limitations."

Athletes and artists who explore the edges of physical limits with their bodies remind us that human beings are fearfully and wonderfully made indeed. They clothe

Exerting and Resting the Body

the mystery of the body in the vivid garment of their disciplined, striving flesh. Watching them, we are inspired to test the limits of our own bodies and our own lives. No wonder the apostle Paul so often draws on the image of the athlete to inspire new Christians to embrace their path with rigor, singleness of purpose, self-control, perseverance, and endurance. No wonder the prophets used images of physical strength to describe the coming reign of God. "Strengthen the weak hands, make firm the feeble knees." When God's people return to Zion, Isaiah writes, "the lame shall leap like a deer" (Isaiah 35:3, 6a).

Any act of exertion might remind us that we are fearfully and wonderfully made. But sometimes we need to remind ourselves of the hidden capacities of our bodies in order to call upon the strength we need. My friend Kay was driving home down the highway that links Oklahoma City and Tulsa after several weeks of caring for her mother, when a tire went flat on her car. It was a windy, cold evening, just after the first frost of the season, and in her haste to get home for a long-awaited meal with her husband, she had jumped into the car without a coat. As the big sky over Oklahoma darkened and the trucks roaring past rattled her tiny car, she did something she had not done since she was sixteen years old, when her father had made her ability to change a tire the condition for keeping a newly acquired drivers license: she got the car jack and lug wrench out of the trunk and set to work. "I *praise* you," she yelled into the wind with each jerk of the wrench, "for I am *fear*fully and *won*derfully made!"

She had spent two weeks tending to her mother,

watching her struggle to marshal all the strength of her body and spirit to fight the cancer that was killing her. Sitting with her mother, Kay had seen the body's vulnerability and strength in equal portions. Now, out on the turnpike, she cried out the body's mystery to God. "I *praise* you," she shouted, and each lug nut loosened. "I am *fear*fully and *won*derfully *made!*" she cried, and her body responded, convinced of its strength. The old tire came off, and she fastened the spare tire in place. She continued her journey home, newly aware of her body, inhabiting every muscle, every cell, every vein. Wishing so much she could give her strength to her mother. Wide awake.

BEING WHERE THE BODY IS

You don't have to be a world-class athlete to experience the pleasure of embodiment through vigorous exertion. You have only to embrace some activity that allows you to feel your heart beating, your blood pulsing, your breath drawn in and released.

For Henry David Thoreau, walking was more than his exertion of choice; it was "the enterprise and adventure of the day." In an essay devoted to walking, he wrote, "I think that I cannot preserve my health and spirits unless I spend four hours a day at least—and it is commonly more than that—sauntering through the woods and over the hills and fields, absolutely free from all worldly engagements."

Exerting and Resting the Body

A nineteenth-century man of letters, with no children to care for and the resources of family and friends to depend upon, Thoreau had time for such walks; most of us don't. But he has something important to teach us about exertion. "I am alarmed when it happens that I have walked a mile into the woods bodily, without getting there in spirit," he writes. "The thought of some work will run in my head and I am not where my body is—I am out of my senses. In my walks I would fain return to my senses."

Being where the body is. Returning to our senses. If we are going to honor our bodies, we must first learn to live in the awareness of blood and bone and breath. But so often, as Thoreau says, we are not where our bodies are. For all of us, vivid consciousness of our body eventually breaks into our lives, and not always in happy ways. Bodily suffering—illness, violence—forces our body upon our attention. When we are in pain, we cannot help but be where our body is. When we are ill, it is impossible to ignore the many ways our body is vulnerable. When we are in danger, it is difficult to remember our body's hidden strength, more difficult still if we have never before called upon it.

Bodily exertion offers a way to learn to live in the consciousness of our body, to learn to be where our body is. But unless our livelihood depends upon manual labor, we must *choose,* deliberately, to exert ourselves. "Here come the joggers," writes Galway Kinnell in his poem "The Tragedy of Bricks."

HONORING THE BODY

They run for fun through a world where everyone
   used to lay bricks
   for work.
Their faces tell there is a hell and they will reach it.

Physical labor has been so thoroughly excised from many of our lives that our bodies have to relearn how to meet the demands of physical activity. We often grimace through our attempts at exertion, like Kinnell's joggers, forcing our bodies into exercise that promises no result as tangible or useful as a brick wall well laid. If we are not exerting our bodies in the dignity of work, we will have to find dignity in exerting our bodies in order to honor and care for them and to strengthen them to care for others.

According to the Surgeon General's 1996 Report on Physical Activity and Health, "only 22 percent of adults . . . are physically active for at least half an hour a day." Most of us are physically active for *less than half an hour a day*. Can that be? Think about your own day and decide. So much of contemporary life conspires against human exertion. Many suburbs are built without sidewalks. Unless you live in a city, you probably have to get in your car to do the simplest things: to go to the store for a carton of milk, or to take your child to a park, or to go to the movies.

There are many good reasons to seek to be where our body is through physical exertion. Sedentary people, as contemporary American culture has proven, tend to become unhealthy people. When we spend a lot of time in our cars and in front of the computer and the TV, we spend less time walking and running and dancing and biking. And we are passing that sedentariness on to our children, who struggle with weight gain and its attendant ill health at younger and younger ages. If we want to honor our bodies and teach our children to honor theirs, we will have to learn how to sustain the natural delight we take in movement when we are young across the whole of our lives.

We honor our bodies as God's creation when we inhabit them with greater attention, for when we are where our body is, we are also where our creator is. The young athlete making a basket from his wheelchair, the disabled woman who lifts weights each day, the man walking the labyrinth with attention, the child who skates up and down her driveway, the marathoner, the rock climber, the quiet beach walker—all have access to the mystery of the body that those of us sitting on our couches in front of the TV do not have. When we reach and stretch and move, we have an opportunity to know ourselves fashioned by one who cherishes bodies. Just as studying a work of art can bring us into the presence, however mediated, of the artist, so attending to our bodies can bring us into the presence of the creator. When we look closely at a painting, we follow the artist's eye as she looks out across a field, or gazes deeply into another's face. We follow her line, her brush stroke, the curve of the clay, and we are, for a moment, in her mind, looking at the world with intensity, making decisions about how to speak of that world with paint or charcoal, bronze or ink. When we reach for a basketball, or speed up at the end of a run, or dance with a child, we have the opportunity to rest for a moment in the mind of God, who formed each of us, each muscle, each tendon, each hair on our head. We have the opportunity to catch a glimpse of the love that makes the body possible. We have the opportunity to see ourselves as God sees us, a beloved creation, fearfully and wonderfully made.

Body as Task or Gift?

It is possible, however, to work at the exertion of our bodies in ways that do not reveal the body as a mystery and a gift, fashioned by God with love. There is a way of embracing exertion that treats the body more as a task than as a gift, a way of allowing what Joan Jacobs Brumberg calls "the body project" to dominate our lives. For every athlete who has sensed the wholeness of the body in the exertions of her sport, there are plenty of others who feel oppressed by the demands made on their bodies, the pressure to keep the body in a particular shape. Whenever we learn that an athlete has been caught taking performance-enhancing drugs that help increase muscle growth in the short term, but in the long term damage the body in lasting ways, we sense the desperation and the pressure to excel that athletics can inspire. And not just big-time athletics. Steroid use is found among high school athletes as well. In pursuit of a more sculpted body, even adolescent boys and (increasingly) girls risk stunted growth, high blood pressure, liver tumors, and a host of other health problems.

Of course, you don't have to participate in organized sports to experience the pressure to build a more perfect body. If we exert our bodies not out of joy or the desire to keep ourselves strong and healthy or the longing to glimpse God's creating hand, but solely out of a desire to perfect our bodies, exertion can become drudgery that forever disappoints or an obsession that diminishes our lives. For although we are indeed fearfully and wonderfully made, we are none of us perfect and never will be, no matter how many magazines promise a PERFECT BODY IN SIX EASY EXERCISES! HAVE THE BODY OF YOUR DREAMS IN TEN DAYS! WASHBOARD ABS! BUNS OF STEEL! BUILD AN IRON-HARD BODY IN JUST FIFTEEN MINUTES A DAY!

How do we honor our body without putting the appearance of our body before every other consideration? How do we resist turning the exertion of our bodies into a task rather than a celebration of a gift beyond price?

I think Thoreau can help us here. Because when we try to be where the body is in all our exertions, we develop a consciousness about our body, an attention to it. We remind ourselves that our body is not something we put on and take off but is instead an indispensable part of who we are. Living in the consciousness that we are our bodies, that our bodies are the gift by which we have life, we can resist simply putting our body through its paces with no attention to its needs or pleasures or limits. We will be, I think, more interested in caring for it, in stewarding its energies, than we will be in perfecting it.

When we start hurting ourselves in service of our vision of what our body should be or look like or do, then we are in danger. The anorectic pounding out mile after mile in her running shoes with no nourishment in her system to sustain her and the young man who ignores the side effects of the steroids he is taking to build his muscles and improve his performance on the playing field are punishing their bodies, treating them as tools to be manipulated, as something other than who they themselves are. But when their body weakens, they will weaken. If their body dies, they will die. It is an age-old tension, this tension between being a body and having a body, and it is all too easy to experience ourselves as merely inhabiting a shell of flesh. It is part of the blessing of exertion that it can restore to us a sense of body and spirit intertwined.

Physical exertion, especially through manual labor, has long been regarded as holy work by many religious traditions. The ritualized running of Native Americans, the climbing of mountains by those seeking to draw near to God, the manual labor of monks—all serve to open a space in which human beings can reach out toward the divine with their bodies. "When they live by the labor of their hands, as our fathers and the apostles did," St. Benedict wrote in his rule for monastic communities, "then they are really monks."

Exerting and Resting the Body

In our sedentary age, some are longing again to seek God with their bodies. The ancient prayer tradition of "walking the labyrinth" has attracted a great deal of interest in the last decade or so. The Rev. Lauren Artress of Grace Cathedral in San Francisco helped retrieve this discipline when she had a duplicate made, in carpet, of the labyrinth found in the floor of Chartres Cathedral, placed it inside Grace Cathedral, and invited people to come, take off their shoes, and walk the path, into the center and out again. "The sheer act of walking a complicated path—which discharges energy—begins to focus the mind," she writes. "Over the months that I have been using the labyrinth as a meditation discipline, there seems to be a cumulative benefit. I feel more focused, more spacious within, and more responsive to the people I encounter in my life."

Perhaps you have never walked a sacred labyrinth. But if you have taken a long, quiet walk in the woods, or along the shore, or through the streets of a city you love, you know what Rev. Artress means.

Another way to resist living as if our body is a task we must complete and perfect is to choose to exert ourselves in ways that bring us joy. I have had many good examples of this in my life: my father, digging and planting all day in the backyard; my husband, rising at dawn to swim in Lake Michigan; my mother, running through the streets of our neighborhood; my daughter, dancing.

I myself belong to the Henry David Thoreau school of joyful exertion: I love to walk. If I could, I'd walk four hours a day, every day, as Thoreau says he did. But who has four hours a day for walking? I have one hour, at the most, so I do what is called speed walking—speed being a relative term, of course. It's speedier than the kind of walking I would do had I four hours each day to do it in, which is to say, I'd walk like a camel, "the only beast," Thoreau wrote, "which ruminates when walking." But since I can't regularly camel-walk through the woods and along the beaches of New England as Thoreau did (sigh), I do what I can. I walk fast for half an hour, I run for ten minutes or so, and then I use the last twenty minutes for a more camel-like pace. I get the aerobic exercise my body needs and the more leisurely sense of my body out and about in creation that my spirit craves. Choosing those exertions that will give us joy doesn't mean we shouldn't challenge ourselves or press against our limits. Indeed, we should. But our exertions shouldn't be all hell-bound grimacing like those of Galway Kinnell's joggers. We should expect to find some pleasure waiting for us when we rouse our bodies to exercise.

Perhaps the best way to resist turning our bodies into projects to be worked on through our exertions is to exert ourselves on behalf of others. It is easy to become absorbed in the workings of one's body when one is alone: *my* heart rate, *my* mileage, *my* speed, *my* weight. Spending a day sanding the walls of a Habitat for Humanity house, or stacking canned goods in a food pantry, or walking with children to and from school through neighborhoods where children are not always safe are also excellent ways to exert the body, to press against its limits, and to attend to its strengths—by making those

Exerting and Resting the Body

strengths available to others. I know of a father of a disabled child who runs each day and lifts weights several times a week so that even when he has grown old, he will be able to lift his daughter from her wheelchair, carry her to the car, settle her into the bath. Offering the gift we have received—the gift of our body—to others makes of our exertion a prayer.

REST AND REFRESHMENT

We also resist the tyranny of the body project when we rest our bodies. I saw a great bumper sticker the other day: "The Labor Movement: the folks who brought you the weekend." We often forget that workers are the ones who have struggled for the right to rest, the right to cease from labor on a regular basis. In the "new economy," which churns along twenty-four hours a day, the gains of workers are newly imperiled and their voices are drowned out in the clamor of profit making and profit taking. But who better understands the body's need for rest than those who work the hardest? Who better to teach the world about the life-giving rhythms of exertion and rest than those who desire both enough work and enough rest? As all workers know, exertion and rest belong together, need each other. They are two parts of one whole. Without exertion, rest is not rest, it is paralysis. And exertion without rest is slavery.

In the Hebrew Bible, God is imagined as the

HONORING THE BODY

worker par excellence, a creator who labors for six days to bring the world and all its creatures into being. In the first three chapters of Genesis alone, God forms, separates, plants, waters, creates human beings, makes their garments, and clothes them. God is artisan and artist, tailor and caregiver, farmer and potter and teacher. This God, this diligent and careful worker, invites us to balance our own days on a rhythm of exertion and rest.

God's own work is punctuated by contemplative moments of rest, in which God gazes upon what God has made and sees that it is good. God brings light into being; God pauses to see that it is good. God creates the flowering earth; God pauses to see that it is good. God's work is not uninterrupted labor, continuous exertion. God's way of working is unrushed, thoughtful, appreciative of what is emerging. Every exertion draws its strength from a profound desire for more life.

Not only does God build a restful pause into the act of creation itself, God weaves into the fabric of the world an entire day of rest, a holy day. "And on the seventh day God finished the work that he had done, and he rested on the seventh day from all the work that he had done. So God blessed the seventh day and hallowed it, because on it God rested from all the work that he had done in creation" (Genesis 2:2–3).

Observance of this holy day of rest becomes a commandment in the books of Exodus and Deuteronomy— one of the ten commandments. In Exodus, the people of Israel are instructed to refrain from work on the sabbath day in order to remember God's own rest after the labor of creation and to honor God's consecration of the day itself. In Deuteronomy, the observance of the sabbath is linked to God's deliverance of Israel from slavery in Egypt. As Dorothy Bass has noted, observance of the sabbath, one day of rest, week after week for a lifetime, is a witness against slavery and a testament to God's desire that all creation be free. For only free people can take a day off. "Sabbath rest," writes Bass, "is a recurring testimony against the drudgery of slavery."

And slavery, as we learn every time we open a newspaper, is not a thing of the past, not even in our own country, where the traffic in human beings often finds a market. The garment workers in El Monte, California, forced to work sixteen hours a day behind razor wire, the immigrant from Thailand hired as a maid and forced to serve her employers' guests on her knees, the thirteen-year-old Vietnamese girl a Silicon Valley executive tried to buy from her parents—all bear witness to the tragic fact that the freedom God desires for all is not yet a reality.

The people of Israel, who knew firsthand that nothing dishonors body and spirit more than slavery, received this commandment, and Jewish people have been living within it ever since, in times of plenty and in times of want, at home and in exile. "More than the Jews have kept *Shabbat, Shabbat* has kept the Jews," the familiar saying goes. Often in the midst of very busy lives, many Jews continue to receive the holy day week after week by putting work aside, gathering at home with family, and sharing prayers and food and refreshment. Each Friday at my daughter's Jewish preschool, the children help bake challah and light candles. They learn to sing ancient prayers in an ancient language. They greet their teachers and one another with *"Shabbat shalom!"*

And school lets out early. Although I am not Jewish, every Friday I remember that the sabbath is coming, because I have to pick up my daughter an hour early. This is not always convenient. But precisely because it is not, it nudges me into awareness that my daughter's teachers, along with others across our city and country and world, need time to make their final preparations to welcome the sabbath: to bathe their children and themselves, to dress in clean and festive clothes, to help each other prepare a clean house and a delicious meal so that, when the sun goes down, they will be ready to cease from working, to light the candles and say the prayers, to sit down together and begin to relax into the rest to which God invites them, week after busy week. I'm told by my observant Jewish friends that preparations do not always go perfectly, the house and the children are not always as clean as one might hope, and worries over work can persist past sundown. But even so, the sabbath beckons them to enter, and by the time three stars appear in the sky on Saturday night (the traditional way of marking the end of the sabbath), they have truly rested. The great poet of the sabbath, Abraham Joshua Heschel, once wrote, "The Sabbaths are our great cathedrals." With the sabbath, Heschel taught, Jews are sustained by holiness in time. Wherever one is on Friday evening, the sabbath opens its great doors and invites one into God's own rest.

To embrace a rhythm of exertion and rest honors

Exerting and Resting the Body

the body in a very real way. Of course, in a world in which many work without moving very much, at desks and computers or before cash registers or conveyer belts, exertion in the form of exercise may *be* a form of rest. If you spend your day moving paper around on a desk, your body may long for the rest and refreshment of a long walk, a bicycle ride, or a run. Centuries of Jewish interpretation of the sabbath have emphasized that the rest offered by the sabbath should be a refreshment for the body as well as for the soul. Eating delicious food, making love, wearing beautiful clothes are all good to do on the sabbath. "Comfort and pleasure," writes Heschel, "are an integral part of the Sabbath observance."

The wisdom of centuries of Jewish sabbath keeping teaches that the sabbath is a time to rest from making, buying, and selling, from profits and losses and the worry they inspire. "Rest even from the thought of labor," some rabbis have taught. But Heschel insists that such rest is not about readying oneself for more labor. "The Sabbath is a day for the sake of life. Man is not a beast of burden, and the Sabbath is not for the purpose of enhancing the efficiency of his work." The sabbath is a good end in itself.

Do Christians keep sabbath? Are we also called to observe a holy day? Certainly we are. But Christian practice (with the exception of Seventh Day Adventists, who keep sabbath on Saturday) over time made Sunday, the day his followers encountered the risen Jesus, the day of sabbath observance. At its best, Christian observance of this day is full of worship and rest and joy, a day on which the body is honored as a holy creation of God, a day on which we can speak and sing our gratitude for life, a day on which we lay aside patterns of consumption in order to learn to taste and see that the Lord is good. As many people who grew up with a strict sabbath practice will tell you, however, Christian sabbath observance can also be stifling, if children are not allowed to run and play, if laughter and boisterousness are frowned upon. Christian sabbath practice can miss the gift of sabbath in other ways as well, especially if Sunday worship is squeezed into an overloaded schedule rather than surrounded by a spaciousness into which our praise can grow.

We live in busy times. Even children have busy schedules, even children often lack the sleep and the rest they need. The balance of exertion and rest that God calls us to promises both enough exertion and enough rest. When we live in the consciousness of the gift of our bodies, both exertion and rest can open a space for contemplation and praise of the mystery that called us into being. We celebrate creation when we honor our bodies and the bodies of others. We celebrate creation as we challenge our bodies' limits through exertion and when we sink into delicious rest when our bodies are tired. We celebrate creation when we offer our strength to another. We celebrate creation when we work on behalf of those who do not have enough work and those who are enslaved and allowed no rest. We celebrate creation when we pause within our exertion to see if it is good. We celebrate creation when we pause once each week from our labors and share in God's own rest.

Our bodies receive rest and refreshment most deeply in sleep, but Americans are notoriously sleep deprived. We get by on the least amount of sleep possible—much less than our bodies need—because we seem not to have *time* for sleeping. In a culture that celebrates achievement and gain, a commitment to getting eight or more hours of sleep each night can be viewed as a sign of lack of ambition, or even laziness. Some cultures structure time for napping into the rhythms of the workday. But even the tradition of the siesta is losing its hold in places where the twenty-four-hour-a-day economy has imposed American work habits.

Our children are often the most sleep deprived of all, especially our teenagers, whose bodies require, but rarely get, ten hours of sleep a night. We all know through experience that when we haven't had enough sleep, we can't think as clearly, or drive as safely. But now researchers tell us that not only does our lack of sleep impair our ability to think and operate the large machinery of our cars, it also impedes the body's ability to defend itself against infections and might contribute to the development of obesity, diabetes, and high blood pressure. Sleep researchers warn that chronic lack of sleep may harm our bodies as much as smoking. We cannot honor our bodies and deprive ourselves of sleep at the same time.

The psalmist writes, "It is vain that you rise early and go late to rest, eating the bread of anxious toil; for

God gives sleep to his beloved" (Psalm 127:2). Sleep is a gift God gives us, a gift that replenishes our bodies, renews our minds, and offers us the opportunity to begin life again every time we awaken. The psalmist reminds us that we of the new economy are not the only ones to have sacrificed sleep to "anxious toil." Anxiety has always been the enemy of sleep.

Just like eating, sleep is a natural bodily process that nevertheless must be learned and taught; anyone who has ever tried to help a child learn to release himself or herself to sleep knows this. I have always tended toward insomnia myself. The least bit of worry will keep me tossing and turning until the wee hours. Even as a child, I had trouble giving myself over to sleep. My parents had a way of helping me fall asleep that I still use today, a method our family called Toes Relax. My mom or dad would lie down next to me in bed and whisper, "Toes relax." I'd think about my toes, flex them a bit, and whisper back, "Toes relax." Then we'd work our way up my body: ankles relax, legs relax, knees relax, thighs relax, bottom relax, tummy relax—all the way up to my head. We'd put my body to sleep, part by part. And it usually worked. By the end of Toes Relax, I'd have flexed and released and bid goodnight to every inch of my body. In the dark, my parents whispered a blessing over every part of me: the blessing of rest, the blessing of the sleep that God wants us to enjoy.

When we are asleep, we are as undefended as it is possible to be. No wonder so many children struggle with learning to sleep. The more we become aware of the dangers in the world, the more difficult it becomes to relax at night. We want to be vigilant, not vulnerable. I have a friend who has devoted much time to teaching her daughters to let go of their day and embrace sleep each night. She believes that by teaching her daughters to sleep, she is teaching them to die. She believes that by teaching them to sleep now, she is giving them a gift that she hopes will one day allow them to relax into God's own care without fear.

In the book of Genesis (28:10–17), Jacob discovers that the place of greatest vulnerability turns out to be the place where earth and heaven meet. On the run from his brother Esau, who is consoling himself for Jacob's theft of his inheritance with thoughts of murderous revenge, Jacob finally stops, exhausted, puts his head on a stone, and falls asleep. In this undefended posture, he finds that he has stretched out his body at the point of intersection between earth and heaven, a place busy with angels. With his head on a stone, asleep under the open sky, with no one watching over him, no walls around him, Jacob finds that God has come to stand beside him. God's voice did not reach him in his desperate search for shelter. Only when he abandons himself to the gift of sleep does he hear what God intends his life to mean.

"God gives sleep to his beloved," the psalmist sings. God desires our rest. For every day is a new day, to be received with joy, an opportunity to try again to become the people God means us to be. An opportunity to encounter, in the needs of our bodies and the bodies of others, the presence of the living God.

Chapter 8

HONORING THE SEXUAL BODY

———

One late afternoon, as dusk began to mute the autumn colors painted across my neighborhood, I caught a glimpse of a good-looking man on a bicycle, waiting for the light to change at an intersection. Sitting in my car at the stoplight, I noticed the long, lanky figure with one leg thrown over his bicycle and the other planted in the street. He was wearing khaki pants, a white shirt, a reddish tie. Was it something about the way he stood? His long legs? The energy contained within his waiting? I'm not sure what it was, but it was something to which my body immediately responded. I felt a certain tightness in my abdomen, a certain fullness. For the last hour I had been driving home to Chicago from the university in Indiana where I taught. My mind was distracted and scattered after a long day, but my body, evidently, was wide awake and attentive. I felt the kindling of sexual desire in spite of myself.

The light changed, and I watched as the man lifted himself back onto his bike and began to ride away. And then I realized that he was my husband.

Looking back, it seems to me a mark of the life we were living then that I hadn't recognized him at first. In our eighth year of marriage, we were living apart for the first time. I taught five days a week in Indiana and spent two or three nights a week there. My husband had just begun a new job teaching in a Roman Catholic theological school in Chicago. We were both deeply involved with new work, new institutions, new students, new colleagues. Having spent the first several years of our marriage as graduate students at the same school, sharing teachers, friends, and books, as well as a bed, we were now, in our first real teaching jobs, leading newly separate lives.

Wrapped in thoughts of the concerns and pleasures of a day that had not included him, I did not immediately recognize the handsome man, leaning forward on his bicycle, waiting for the light to change. But my body did. My body responded to what it knew and cherished —the body of my husband, a body that is for me harbor and refuge, strength and comfort, source of the very deepest pleasure.

When the light changed, I watched him pedal east, which meant that he was going back to his office, probably to work for an hour or two more before heading home. I knew I had time to take a shower and brush my teeth before he returned. I knew I had time to put to-

gether a simple supper, open a bottle of wine. I knew I
had time to straighten the house a bit, light some candles,
close the blinds. The warmth inside me spreading, I
drove home to prepare myself to get reacquainted with
a man who was, and is to this day, both familiar and un-
familiar, both mysterious and known.

FREEDOM AND DESIRE

The mystery of sexual desire—the way it can flood us
unexpectedly—is something over which philosophers
and religious thinkers have long ruminated. For if desire
can well up without our intending it, then exactly how
free are we? The "tyranny of desire," bemoaned in much
ancient philosophy, was something to be mastered by
training one's reason to have control over the body's appetites. It was my distracted and scattered mind, Plato
would no doubt have argued, that allowed me to be sur-
prised by sexual desire as I sat at the stoplight.

Early Christians also worried over how they might
gain control over the body's unruly desires. The apostle
Paul counseled celibacy but argued for marriage if sexual desire could not be kept in check: "it is better to
marry," he famously wrote, "than to burn" (I Corinthians 7:9). The message that marriage provided an acceptable way to organize one's sexual desires but that celibacy
was the higher path was received loudly and clearly by
later Christians. Wanting to be the finest Christian he
could possibly be, St. Augustine would not consent to be

baptized until he felt himself able to embrace that path. His conversion is, in part, a seduction by Lady Continence, who appeared to him as he struggled with whether or not he could give up sexual relationships, "enticing me to come to her without hesitation, stretching out to receive and to embrace me with those holy hands of hers." It is only when he is sure he can live without sex that he becomes a Christian.

Is there anything to be learned about honoring the sexual body from early Christians like Paul and Augustine, who believed that the highest human calling was a celibate one? Certainly their perspectives took shape within a culture marked by unequal relations between men and women. Certainly those perspectives helped shape a religious culture in which the desires of the body were viewed with suspicion, a culture that bequeathed to us a fear of desire that persists to this day.

But I think it is possible also to hear in the words of Paul and Augustine not only a suspicion of the body but also an honest acknowledgment of the power of sexual desire, a struggle to understand their vulnerability to it, and a real desire for freedom. It is possible, as Augustine knew, to be imprisoned by one's desires and to become locked in patterns of satisfying them that make use of others as a means of one's satisfaction only. It is possible to be led by one's desires away from one's most profound aspirations, from the life one hopes to lead.

There have been times in Christian history when the refusal of sexual relationships meant the refusal to believe in the goodness of the body. But there have also been times when Christians have refused sexual relationships in order to preserve their freedom. When some early Christians, men and women alike, decided to live outside of the institutions of marriage and family, they declared that their bodies belonged to God, not the Roman Empire, for whom the body and its desires were tools for empire building. When these early Christians chose sexual abstinence in order to preserve their life's energies for prayer and service, they generated no new citizens, no new soldiers, no new cities. They shocked their contemporaries by becoming so "useless." By claiming their bodies and their desires for God, they claimed them for themselves. They claimed the freedom to make their own choices about the currents in which their desires would run, the uses to which their bodies would be put.

For women, sexual abstinence has sometimes been one of the few roads leading to freedom. The history of Christianity is full of stories of women who run to the monastery or the hermitage or the anchorhold to escape the marriages arranged for them by their parents and to embrace a life of prayer, study, and service. In an age when women married young to men not of their choosing, whose bodies were worn out early by the hard work of frequent childbearing, the celibacy practiced in women's religious communities meant not the end of freedom but the beginning of it—freedom to seek God, to become educated, to read and write, to preach and teach. And judging from the writings of some of these women, in which the desire for God is described in

Honoring the Sexual Body

deeply erotic terms, it by no means required an end to engagement with the sexual dimension of the self.

In our day, when "sexual freedom" seems to signify only multiple sexual partners, it is good to remember that postponing or refusing sexual relationships can also be a gesture toward freedom. It is good for young people, whose sexual selves are still unfolding, to know that delaying full sexual expression might preserve for them the freedom to live into a deeply satisfying sexual life as adults. It is good for couples practicing the discipline of sexual fidelity to remember the freedom that unfolds over time when two people remain committed to one another's pleasure in a context of trust and faithfulness. It is good for those living with—or without—a sexual relationship to remember that the erotic dimension of life is not dependent on sexual intercourse. "The erotic," as the work of the poet Audre Lorde teaches, "is that which allows us deep connection with others, giving joy, creative energy, and the capacity for feeling; that which empowers persons to change the world; that which is the deep yes within the self." It is good for all of us to remember that such a rich understanding of the erotic can only flourish in freedom.

ECSTASY

But are nervous worries over how sexual desire might rob us of our freedom the only resource we have for constructing a Christian practice that honors the body's desires? Is "it is better to marry than to burn" the only guidance the Bible gives us for honoring our sexuality? By no means! Sometimes the Bible is clear that it is quite wonderful to burn.

"Let him kiss me with the kisses of his mouth!" So opens the most erotic book of the Bible, the Song of Solomon, or, as it is sometimes called, the Canticle of Canticles, the Song of Songs. In this long poem lying at the heart of scripture between the pragmatic Ecclesiastes and the sublime Isaiah, a woman, "black and beautiful," and a man, "radiant and ruddy," speak the language of desire, cataloguing every inch of each other's body, every smell and taste. "Your navel is a rounded bowl that never lacks mixed wine," he says to her (7:2). "His cheeks are like beds of spices, yielding fragrance. His lips are lilies, distilling liquid myrrh," she tells her friends (5:13). "Your two breasts," he sings, "are like two fawns, twins of a gazelle" (7:3). "I am my beloved's," she exults, "and his desire is for me" (7:10).

The Song of Songs is a song about desire, and so it is also a song about the pain of separation, of missed meetings, of absence. "O that his left hand were under my head," the woman sings with palpable yearning, "and that his right hand embraced me!" (2:6). Describing a moment when her lover knocked on her door and she hesitated for a moment to open, the woman speaks some of the sexiest lines in any literature.

My beloved thrust his hand into the opening,
and my inmost being yearned for him.

Honoring the Sexual Body

I arose to open to my beloved,
and my hands dripped with myrrh,
my fingers with liquid myrrh,
upon the handles of the bolt [5:4–5].

When she opens the door, however, he is gone, and she heads out into the city to search for him.

I adjure you, O daughters of Jerusalem,
if you find my beloved,
tell him this:
I am faint with love [5:8].

How did this erotic love poem make it into the Bible? No one knows for sure. But scores of interpreters, both Jewish and Christian, have found in it the song of the human yearning for God and God's desire to be in relationship with humanity. The Song of Songs is read at the festival of the Passover as a reminder that God delivered Israel from slavery not only because God was contractually bound to do so through the covenant but also because God loved the people of Israel and desired their good. The Christian writer Bernard of Clairvaux wrote more than eighty sermons on Song (never getting past the third chapter!), and found in the poem a means by which the individual person could come into intimate relationship with God. St. John of the Cross discovered in the Song the inspiration for his own poetry, a poetry of absence and longing that describes how "the dark night of the soul" is an organic and potentially fruitful moment in the human search for God.

Like all great poetry, the Song of Songs can easily sustain such a range of interpretations. But it also resists being read *only* as a spiritual text about human beings and God (as Bernard of Clairvaux well knew when he counseled that young monks and nuns should not be allowed to read it until their faith had matured, because of the sexual feelings it was able to inspire). From the pages of scripture sacred to Jews and Christians alike, the Song of Songs remains a testimony to mutuality in love, to the beauty of the human body, to the goodness of sexual desire and the power of love: "Love is as strong as death," the Song proclaims, "passion fierce as the grave."

> Many waters cannot quench love,
> neither can floods drown it.
> If one offered for love all the wealth of his house,
> it would be utterly scorned [8:6–7].

In the Song of Songs we find no anxiety about desire's power to deny us the freedom to be who God intends us to be. In the Song of Songs, desire is portrayed as Mark Doty describes it in his meditation on the death of his lover, Wally Roberts: "the ineradicable force that binds us to the world." The relationship described in the Song is one of mutuality; the lovers are evenly matched in the force of their desire. They are equally vulnerable in their desire to *be* desired by the other; they are equally determined to give and receive pleasure. "I will hasten to the mountain of myrrh," he says to her, "and the hill of frankincense" (4:6). "I would give you spiced wine to drink," she responds, "the juice of my pomegranates"

Honoring the Sexual Body

(8:2). In the Song, desire leads not to exploitation but rather, as Doty says, to "participation, the will to involve oneself in the body of the world, in the principle of things expressing itself in splendid specificity, a handful of images: a lover's irreplaceable body, the roil and shimmer of sea overshot with sunlight, a handful of cherries, the texture and weight of a word."

Through desire, Doty writes, "we are implicated in another being, which is always the beginning of wisdom, isn't it?" What a wonderful way to account for why the Song of Solomon appears in the wisdom literature of the Bible and why it ought to matter to us as we construct a Christian practice of honoring the body. Because it shows us a path, through desire, outside the boundaries of our individual selves. Because it offers a way of receiving the world that is motivated by love and speaks of God's own passionate creativity. Because it teaches that in seeking the pleasure of another we may find our own deepest pleasure and in the commitment to another we may come to know ecstasy.

SHELTERING THE EVOLVING SEXUAL SELF

Isn't this what we want for ourselves and our children? Relationships so intimate and satisfying that they draw us out of ourselves and more deeply into the life of the world? Relationships in which pleasure is given and received with joy? Relationships in which knowledge of the body is sought with care and gentleness, in which the body is pronounced beautiful over and over again?

I remember a long-ago conversation with a friend, the mother of two sons. "I hope they will grow up to be good lovers," she told me. I was too immature at the time to understand what a profound hope that was, too young to understand what she was teaching me about being a parent. Her sons are grown now, and I imagine her hope has been realized. For when she and her husband spoke to their sons about sex, which they did freely and often, they did not give them a list of unexplained do's and don'ts. When they set limits, they set them in the context of their hope that their sons would one day know deep sexual satisfaction with someone whose life and body and spirit they cherished.

As these parents knew, the path to adult sexual satisfaction is treacherous. Negotiating adolescence is so difficult, so full of pitfalls. In our first encounters with desire—our own and others'—we might entrust ourselves to someone who is not careful with our bodies or with our spirits. We might imperil our freedom through entering into the entanglement of a sexual relationship too early in life, or through fathering a child, or through becoming pregnant. We might be preyed upon by someone bent on exploitation. Bad early sexual experience is so wounding, so difficult to recover from. How can we help young people thread a path through their early years that is spacious enough to develop deep and loving relationships with others but narrow enough to preserve their sexual selves? How can we help them survive bad experiences and go on to live sexually ful-filling lives?

The practice of honoring the body requires us to offer young people homes and friendships, classrooms and churches, in which bodies and their desires are hon-ored and welcomed and discussed. A changing body and the first stirrings of sexual desire can be isolating if there is no safe place in which these changes and stirrings can be acknowledged. Mark Doty, in his memoir about growing up gay in the 1950s, experienced his adolescent body as "a stiff insulating container for my desires, an armor for holding that potential conflagration in check." He remembers praying that he would not get an erection while surrounded by naked boys in his school gym's locker room and having no one to talk to about the storm of feelings he weathered alone. Marya Hornbacher, in her memoir of her struggle with anorexia and bulimia, writes of feeling isolated in and by her body as an ado-lescent: "It was as if people could *see,* just by the very presence of my breasts, that I was bad and sexual and needy. I shrank back from my body as if it were going to devour me."

My breasts began to develop when I was in the sixth grade. A boy in my class noticed this, and began, every time the teacher was out of the room (and that year I had a teacher who used any excuse to get away from us), to come over to my desk and touch me. I was ashamed and in despair over this and would pray at night that he would lose interest in my body. One day, as soon as our teacher left the room, he ran straight over to my desk, grabbed my breast, and ran back to his own seat. When the teacher returned a moment later, she began calling on us to stand before the class to make oral reports. Although I had prepared my report, although I was the kind of kid who always had her assignments done on time, when she called on me I told her I wasn't ready. "You're not *ready?*" I remember her asking incredulously. "No," I said, in an act of self-protection. I was too unsure of myself and too embarrassed to stand up front of the boy who had touched me and the classmates who had laughed as he did.

My teacher never asked me why I didn't get my work done. And it never occurred to me to talk with her about it. That is not surprising, for she was the kind of absent, preoccupied adult who even very young kids know will not protect them. What is more surprising to me is that I never told my parents, never asked for their help. My parents were open and loving. They modeled a healthy relationship that was clearly full of joy and satisfaction. I trusted them completely. But I was too ashamed to go to them with this problem. I remember this now, as a parent, how powerful those feelings of shame are, how even the most loving of parents are sometimes no match for them.

I learned this anew when a friend told me recently that he had been sexually assaulted as a boy by a neighborhood bully. After my friend got away, he walked home, ate his supper, went to bed—and told no one what had happened to him. Not his parents, not his siblings, not his pastor, not his teachers, not his friends. He just went home and began trying to forget.

Honoring the Sexual Body

Where can a young boy like Mark Doty go as his sexual identity begins to take shape? Who will accompany him as he grows in self-knowledge? Who will welcome him as the gay man he is becoming and keep him from becoming one of many gay adolescents who commit suicide? Where can a young girl, confused about her body's desires, go to understand them? Where can she go when her body draws others to her in ways she does not welcome? Where can a young boy go to learn to respect the boundaries of other bodies? Where can a young boy go when he has been terrorized? How can we protect these young people and preserve for them the possibility of sexually fulfilling lives in the future?

Our culture's lore about The Talk that every mother has with her daughter and every father has with his son will not help us here. Not that there doesn't need to be frank talk about sex. But talk that emerges in isolation from the rest of life, talk that happens in one conversation, covers all the bases, and then is dropped forever will probably not make much of a difference in anyone's life. Only talk that arises organically within an ongoing practice of honoring the body can help us make ready homes and churches and communities of all kinds that reverence the gift of sexuality. The sexual body does not exist apart from the body that eats and drinks, bathes and dresses, rests and exercises and works. Sexual desire does not exist in isolation from other desires. It is only through learning to honor the body in every aspect of our embodied life that we will be able to honor our bodies' sexual feelings and desires.

Christian faith bears within it the resources to help us honor our sexual bodies, but these resources will help us only if we engage them in youth groups, in sermons, in Sunday School, in service, in worship, and in the midst of everyday life. Our faith can help us if we are constantly exploring—in our everyday meals and in the Lord's Supper, in bathing and in baptism, in caring for others and in caring for ourselves—what it means that God named all creation good and that God was made present in the body of a human being. Our faith can help us if we pay attention to how God's love of difference is expressed in the many different bodies that grace the earth and how God's care for us is expressed in the sexual intimacy that our God-given bodies make possible.

Children who grow up in communities that consistently articulate the goodness of the body will be better able to resist viewing the body as a source of shame. Churches that greet the image of God in gay bodies and straight bodies, in bodies of all sizes and shapes, all races, all colors, create a harbor for all who are growing into their sexual selves. Teachers and pastors and physicians who really know the children in their care are better able to be attentive to their feelings and their fears than those who hold themselves apart. Parents who delight in their children's bodies and acknowledge their growth and change help bestow a sense of the goodness about the body that can persist over a lifetime. I remember that when I got my period for the first time my dad sat on the side of my bed and told me how proud he was of the woman I was becoming. We were probably both a little embarrassed. But I've never forgotten the gravity of the moment, the seriousness with which my father took me and my body, the respect he believed I and my body were due.

Young people who have grown up learning that the body mirrors back to us something important about God and that the body's desires are a precious gift from God worthy of being sheltered and allowed to develop in freedom have a compass to help them negotiate the road to sexual maturity. Adolescence will never be easy. And our world holds dangers that are sometimes beyond our power to control. But young people who have learned to honor their bodies in every other aspect of their lives will be more convinced that their bodies and the bodies of others are deserving of honor in their sexual lives as well. They will be better equipped to resist that which would diminish them or constrain their freedom to become the people they were meant to be, and better able to embrace that which would enlarge their spirits and nurture an ever more loving engagement with the world.

EXQUISITE CONSOLATION

Adolescents are not the only ones who need the help of loving communities to learn to honor their sexual selves. Adults do as well. Adults also need freedom and shelter, protection and love, as their sexuality unfolds. Adults also need to be convinced of the goodness of their bodies, also need to have their desire for intimate touch answered by the touch of another.

The novelist Martin Amis tells a wonderful story about the mending power of sexual intimacy in his memoir, *Experience*. After years of unrelenting tooth pain and disease, all of his teeth were removed and replaced. In the midst of this long, excruciating process, he had to wear, for several weeks, a prosthetic device that filled his mouth with saliva, made it difficult for him to talk or eat, and made him feel distinctly unlovely and undesirable.

"That night," he writes to his wife of the night after he had been fitted with the false teeth, "you came belly-dancing out of the bathroom wearing (a) your silk bathrobe and (b) my teeth. Both were then removed.

"This was the war against shame.

"The next morning I woke early and lay there quietly laughing and weeping into the pillow. I felt fragile, guileless, and exquisitely consoled."

Fragile, guileless, and exquisitely consoled. That's a pretty good description of how we are rendered by good sex with a loving partner. Fragile, because it is always a risk to expose ourselves, unguarded, to another. Guileless, because, in the deepest sexual encounters, the many ways we defend ourselves—our masks, our self-deceptions— fall away. And exquisitely consoled—ah, yes. To have our desire met and satisfied by the desire of another is exquisitely consoling.

Sex, as a physical act, is not all that complicated. People meet in bars, at conferences, and in on-line chat rooms and pair off for sex all the time. Orgasms are

Honoring the Sexual Body

achieved and certain needs are, however briefly, met. But a casual acquaintance will not come to you as you lie toothless in bed and make love to you in a way that returns to you your best self. Such lovemaking can only be had in a relationship rooted in intimacy and trust.

Sex, on its own, does not guarantee intimacy. The book of Genesis says that when a man leaves his home and cleaves to his wife, they become one flesh, and Jesus repeats these words in the Gospel of Matthew (19:6) to argue against divorce. But is this lovely image really accurate? For no matter how deeply one person enters another in sex, no matter how tightly our limbs intertwine, no matter how long and slow the kisses of the mouth that the Song of Song celebrates, we never do become one flesh with one another, not really. For even when we are as close as it is physically possible to be, it is still possible to keep secrets from one another. It is still possible to lie to one another. It is possible to have sex and never become intimate. Moreover, we cannot feel what our partner feels because we cannot share our partner's flesh. Our bodies allow us to draw near to one another, but they also keep us separate from one another. And so sex, like all moral activity, requires us to imagine what another person feels, to seek what will give pleasure and avoid what will not.

Birth, death, and sex: these are the moments when we are perhaps best able to glimpse the connection between what is vulnerable and what is sacred. For sex that is exquisitely consoling and reflects God's desire for our freedom and our good can only be had when two people

HONORING THE BODY

make themselves vulnerable to one another. It cannot be had when one person is being exploited, it cannot be had when love is withheld, it cannot be had when it is being used as a means to any other end than mutual reverence and delight. What a fine line there is between what heals and what wounds. If it were otherwise, the consolations of sexual intimacy would not be so profound.

Nor would the damage done by the misuse of sex be so bruising. Sex between people who do not love one another and are not willing to become uniquely responsible to and for one another assumes a split between body and spirit that does not exist. When we have sex, all of who we are is on the line. Any attempt to deploy our bodies in a sexual encounter while holding back the rest of our selves damages us; the impossible attempt to divide body and spirit does violence to both. And so the wisdom of the Christian tradition for the honoring of the sexual body has most often been found in its advocacy of the marriage covenant as the best home for sexual intimacy.

COVENANT

In more than a decade as an ordained minister, I can probably count on one hand the number of weddings I have performed in which the couple has never been sexually intimate. Indeed, many of the couples I've married have already established shared households and bank accounts, as well as a shared bed. The truth is, single people are making their way as best they can, often with precious little usable direction from religious institutions about how they should live their sexual lives. Some of them arrive at the altar sexually scarred and wounded; some are veterans of "serial monogamy," now ready to settle down; some of them come sexually healthy and satisfied and looking forward to a deepening of that satisfaction in the years ahead with their partner; some of them are terrified at the thought of pledging their bodies sexually to one person alone.

All of these people, as they prepare to promise to be faithful and present to one another in good times and in bad, stand at the threshold of a Christian vocation that holds great potential for honoring the sexual body: the vocation of marriage. This does not mean that every marriage is a good marriage, or even a sexually satisfying marriage. It means that marriage offers the possibility for intimacy, including sexual intimacy, to deepen and flourish over time in a context of mutual care and fidelity.

Some contemporary couples, wanting to acknowledge this possibility in their wedding ceremonies, have retrieved an old form of the ring ceremony in which the bridegroom would say to the bride as he put the ring on her finger, "With my body I thee worship." In our day this poetic pledge of fidelity has been recovered as words spoken by both partners to acknowledge their pledge to nurture their relationship with sexual love and their commitment to making sex an important expression of the promises they are making to one another.

Christians have not always articulated the relationship between sex and marriage as a way in which married people cared for one another. Many early Christians looked to procreation as the primary motive for sex within marriage, and some Christians still do. The purpose of God's gift of sexual union, many Christians have reasoned, is to make more life. Some Christians viewed marriage as a healing form within which sexual passions could become properly ordered: one could relieve one's sexual urges within the bond of holy matrimony and so free oneself from the temptation to promiscuity. Martin Luther, in a sermon on marriage, tells his congregation that sexual union is the very essence of marriage, and if one partner cannot fulfill his or her conjugal duties (although Luther claims that it is usually the man who fails the woman), he or she imperils the very salvation of the other's soul. A woman whose husband will not or cannot make love to her should try to get her husband to agree to allow her to make a "secret marriage" with a close male relative of her husband, Luther says. If her husband will not agree, she should flee to another country and contract a new marriage there. Sexual desire, says Luther, is a sign of "God's ordinance to multiply," and God's ordinances should not be resisted.

Christian thinking in our day is more likely to stress that sex within marriage is good not only because children might result from it, or because it offers an alternative to promiscuity, but also because it deepens the communion between marriage partners. The Second Vatican Council, while continuing to affirm procreation as the purpose of marriage, also named sexual relations

Honoring the Sexual Body

between married partners as "noble and worthy," one of the forms of "mutual self-giving by which spouses enrich one another." Sex within marriage has come to be honored as the holy gift it is.

But what about sex outside of marriage? Have the churches offered us any guidance here? The United Methodists made a slogan out of a traditional Christian conviction: "Celibacy in singleness, fidelity in marriage." The United Church of Christ offers instead a "principle of proportionality": the level of sexual involvement should not outstrip the level of commitment. A sexual ethic for single people, Christian ethicist Karen Lebacqz argues, should have the protection of vulnerability at its core. For while sex renders all of us vulnerable, single people, she maintains, are uniquely so because they are unprotected by a covenant of fidelity. She believes that the church should provide a consistent witness against sex between unequal partners and at the same time leave room for the practice of pre- and postmarital adult sexual intimacy, in which both partners make themselves vulnerable to the other.

But, of course, if you read the newspapers, you know that the most fiercely fought debates over sexuality in churches these days have to do less with questions of premarital sex and more to do with homosexuality and whether churches ought to bless the union of homosexual partners. In recent years we've seen church trials of pastors who have blessed such relationships and the disfellowshipping of churches that have welcomed gay and lesbian Christians into their congregations. To say that the

HONORING THE BODY

church is struggling with this issue is an understatement. At times we seem to be devouring ourselves over it.

Can the Christian practice of honoring the body help us here? It is, after all, a practice, not a set of doctrines. But can we live as if all bodies are good and then say that some bodies are worthy of condemnation? Can we cherish the discipline of fidelity and then say that it is wrong for some people to live within the bonds of faithful love? Can we insist on the unity of body and spirit and then ask some people to deny their sexuality, to divide an integral part of their identity from their very selves?

The covenant of marriage is one of the finest gifts Christian faith has to offer to those who wish to care for one another, make families with one another, and live in sexual intimacy with one another. Marriage can be a important dimension of the practice of honoring the body, and the practice of honoring the body is indispensable to the flourishing of a marriage. What is crucial is not whether the partners are heterosexual or homosexual. What is crucial is whether there is trust and fidelity, whether vulnerability is shared, and whether a new family formed by covenant is an agent of blessing in the world.

Making a lifetime covenant, speaking a promise one intends to keep in good times and in bad, is a risk for anybody, straight or gay. People will grow and change, as they should. Will the covenant be elastic enough for two people to pursue their different dreams within it? The daily pressures and responsibilities of life lived in covenant will on occasion threaten to overwhelm. Can the marriage remain a harbor, even in times of stress? There will be days of difficulty and confusion. Will the vows exchanged on the wedding day be able to hold out the possibility of intimacy and shared vocation? There will be seasons of intense sexual feeling, and seasons when the erotic energies of one or the other partner seem channeled instead into work or parenting or friendship. Will there be enough generosity in the marriage to allow for this, enough patience to wait until the seasons cycle around again?

And the biggest risk of all, the risk that we all take when we love, is that someone will be left alone when death claims the beloved. I remember the first time in my life when I knew, really knew, that I would one day die. It was the moment when I stood in the back of a church in Chicago and looked down the aisle at my waiting husband-to-be. Suddenly, what we were about to embark upon seemed like one long good-bye.

One of the most famous wedding stories of all is the story of Jesus' first miracle at the wedding at Cana (John 2:1–11), the story in which the host runs out of wine at the wedding feast and Jesus' mother urges her reluctant son to keep the party going, to change a few jars of water into the finest wine. The author of the Gospel of John tells us nothing about the bride and groom—they are left unnamed and undescribed. But even though they are ignorant of the miracle taking place, it is the ordinary miracle of their pledging themselves to one another until death parts them that opens a space for all the other miracles of the day. For it is precisely when two people are led by love to make such radical commitments that the boundaries between earth and heaven, between water and wine, seem so transgressable.

We live by those commitments in so many ways and in so many circumstances—in sickness and in health, in good times and in bad, in wealth and in poverty—until we are parted by death. When we mark those commitments by sexual intimacy and sexual fidelity, when we devote ourselves to learning to meet the desires of our beloved, and when we teach our beloved to answer our body's longing, we taste one of the sweetest gifts God has bestowed.

Chapter 9

HONORING THE SUFFERING BODY

—

Nothing brings the body as rapidly and sharply to our attention as suffering. When we are ill or wounded or in any kind of bodily pain, it is impossible to ignore our bodies.

But while bodily suffering is impossible to ignore, it is nearly as impossible to describe. "The merest school-girl, when she falls in love, has Shakespeare and Keats to speak her mind for her," Virginia Woolf complains, "but let a sufferer try to describe a pain in his head to a doctor and language at once runs dry."

Elaine Scarry, the author of *The Body in Pain,* goes further than Woolf: suffering not only defies language, it also destroys it. Often, when we are in pain, we are able to utter only the sounds we made before we could use or understand language. Putting those preverbal cries into language that can be shared with others requires an additional step of invention and imagination. We have to use the language of "as if" and "it is as though" to communicate our pain to others: "It is as though my head were in a vise," we say. "I feel as if there are nails in my stomach."

Those who would care for suffering bodies must also make a leap of imagination in order to understand and respond to another's pain. The philosopher Simone Weil was fond of reminding her readers that in the first legend of the Holy Grail, the seeker who receives the Grail is the one who asks the vessel's guardian, a badly wounded king, the question "What are you going through?" Weil writes,

> The capacity to give one's attention to a sufferer is a very rare and difficult thing; it is almost a miracle; it *is* a miracle.

Weil is right. It is difficult to give one's whole attention to someone who is suffering. In some ways, honoring the body of a suffering person ought not be very complicated, because the needs of a suffering body are so clear. But, of course, it *is* complicated, because it is painful to observe someone else's suffering, because the suffering of others highlights our own bodily vulnerability, because—and this is perhaps the most difficult of all—we cannot always make that suffering go away. No wonder our culture prefers to honor healthy, whole, beautiful bodies. No wonder we keep suffering bodies well out of sight.

A physician's prayer attributed to the Jewish philosopher Maimonides asks that "in the sufferer let me see only the human being." This simple prayer exposes a profound dilemma. For it is all too easy to see in another's suffering a host of unmanageable symptoms or a glimpse of the bodily failure that we ourselves fear rather than the human being experiencing affliction. The practice of honoring the body seeks to keep the whole human being in view and to reverence the mystery of that person through tending carefully to his or her body.

"I Do Choose"

There is a remarkable institution in Chicago's West Side called Interfaith House, which I have gotten to know through students who have held internships there. It is a place where homeless people who have been ill or injured are cared for after they are discharged from the hospital. It exists because members of the Chicago Interfaith Council for the Homeless understood that healing is not possible if you have no safe place to go to regain your strength, and they worked hard to bring such a place into being. Interfaith House has sixty beds. It is the only place in the Midwest where homeless people can go to recover from illness or injury.

Honoring the Suffering Body

The staff members of Interfaith House believe deeply that the body can be healed only if the whole person is treated with dignity. Residents of Interfaith House are offered food and housing, counseling and financial advice, assistance in finding permanent housing, and, if they wish, the opportunity to participate in daily services of morning prayer and Bible study. For my students, participating in daily morning prayer at Interfaith House has been life changing. Art Bendixen, the program director at Interfaith House, speaks for many of them: "My theology is based on the incarnational mode of Christianity. I really do believe that the closest place you can get to God is through other people. I very much believe that God identifies in a special way with those who suffer most in society. I do find that God is very much present in them. When I participate in morning prayer with them, my whole faith gets challenged. Their commitment, their hope, their faith challenges mine."

Like Maimonides, praying to keep the whole person in view, members of the staff of Interfaith House promote the healing of the persons in their care by treating them with respect. In their speech, they take care to protect the dignity of the residents. When they call a resident over the PA system, they say "please come" rather than "please report." They address each resident by name. They inquire not only into the physical injuries of those in their care but into their spiritual struggles as well. They receive each resident not as a "case" to be "solved" but as a complicated human being whose life is precious. What is deeply understood at Interfaith House is that in order to care for a suffering body one must care for the whole person.

In the Gospel of Mark, Jesus is approached by a leper whose illness has estranged him from the community. "If you choose," he says to Jesus, "you can make me clean." Jesus is moved by this request, stretches out his hand, and touches the man. "I do choose," he says. "Be made clean" (Mark 1:40–41).

The founders and staff of Interfaith House have made such deliberate choices: the choice to seek the face of God in the bodies of the sick and injured, the choice not to turn away from the suffering of others, the choice to offer healing that is more than the reknitting of bones and skin.

These are not easy choices to make. It is not easy to ask someone, "What are you going through?" It is not easy to respond, when asked for help and healing, "I do choose." The practice of honoring the body helps prepare us to make these difficult choices. If we have learned to reverence the body in the ordinary moments of everyday life, we might be better able to keep the sacredness of the body in view even in the midst of suffering.

I can remember, as a child in Sunday School, being taught to be present to those experiencing bodily suffering. Our classes adopted each year a "shut-in," usually an old and infirm person who lived in a nursing home or alone in a tiny apartment. We would visit once a month, bringing gifts we'd made, singing songs we'd learned. We would sit on the floor at the feet of a man or a woman with a chronic illness or an injury that kept him or her homebound. We would touch their papery skin, smell their smells, receive their kisses. Did we know we were being taught to honor the body? No— although we did understand that we were being taught to follow Jesus, to be in the places Jesus wanted us to be. But what remains in my memory are not the songs we sang or the scripture we shared. What remains in my memory are the bodies of those we visited—bodies in wheelchairs, bodies in bandages, bodies that had grown very old. I remember their translucent, trembling hands and the sense that we were in the presence of something a little frightening but very compelling. Frightening, because it gave us a glimpse into what might be our own future. Compelling, because in the midst of visible suffering there was a still a desire on all our parts for connection, for touch, for community. The visits always ended too soon.

In Judaism, *bikur cholim,* visiting the sick, is a commandment required of all. I hope Christians will also work to keep the tradition of visiting the sick alive, especially for children. In an age when we have professionalized so many aspects of life, including the life of faith, it is all too easy to leave visiting the sick to the pastors, the chaplains, the counselors, the social workers. But Jesus said that when we care for those who are sick, we care for him. Arthur Bendixen and the staff of Interfaith House believe this, and so their care is respectful and unrushed. They honor the body by honoring the whole person. Such care takes practice, and we are never too young to begin.

HEALING TOUCH

Whether we are ill or well, our skin is hungry for touch. I realized how much I depended on touch throughout the day when my husband and I lived in Italy for a year during graduate school. I would often go to the cathedral for an evening service before meeting Kevin for dinner, and I found that I looked forward most of all to the passing of the peace. After a day of working in a quiet library, where I knew no one, I longed to touch another person. The ritual of passing the peace offered a safe place in which even strangers could touch one another in kindness and hope.

When we are ill, touch can be healing. A group of friends in a Chicago church responded to this reality when one of them became terminally ill. As he grew sicker, his body first became a stranger and then an enemy to him, a source of nothing but anguish. In the last months of his life, he told his friends of his feeling of having been abandoned by his body. They began reading about and training themselves in therapeutic massage. They began to gather regularly in his home, to stroke his hands and feet, to touch his skin, to offer his body back to him as a source of comfort, not of pain alone. Through these sessions of therapeutic touching, he found himself more able to speak freely about his illness and his inevitable death. Through the practice of touching, his friends found themselves able to respond with compassion rather than fear, with openness rather than denial.

And when their friend died, they found comfort in the healing touch of one another.

That group of friends challenges me to enlarge my understanding of healing. How wonderful it would have been if those friends had touched their dying friend, and his sickness had disappeared. But that didn't happen. He remained sick. And he died. But there was healing in the midst of his illness, healing in a deep sense. Before he died, he was able to experience his body as a good and holy creation. His friends returned his body to him, broken, yet beautiful, a temple of the Holy Spirit still.

A woman in my parents' church recently shared with me a story about a body honored and reverenced by the touch of another. She was led to work with refugees after surviving a bout of breast cancer. So grateful was she for her life that she decided, in her retirement, to offer her skills and her home to others. She has been particularly involved with refugees from Iraq, many of whom are devout Muslims. One man entered this country with a heart condition requiring immediate surgery. She found a doctor who would do the surgery and a hospital that would welcome the man for far less money than was required. Following the surgery, she and one of the refugees who shares her home went to the hospital to visit. When they arrived, the man who had accompanied her asked for a bowl of warm water from the nurses. What could he want with that? she wondered. When the bowl of water arrived, the man sat near the foot of the bed and washed the feet of his fellow countryman. He washed them gently,

HONORING THE BODY

carefully, thoroughly, top and bottom, between each toe.

"I was amazed," she told me, "by the care my friend took with the feet of a complete stranger. But even more, I was amazed that such an act could be a way of *greeting* another person, that it might be possible to *begin* with the body and then move to words. I have learned a great deal from my Muslim friends," she told me, "about honoring the body."

To begin with the body. That is one way of being present to those who suffer that helps us keep the whole human person in view. Whereas it is unusual in this culture for one person to greet another by washing his or her feet, it is not unusual to greet another with an embrace, a kiss, a touch of the hand. The trouble is, these gestures are often so familiar that they are dispensed with quickly and without understanding them as a way of attending to the body of another. Becoming more conscious of "beginning with the body," as this woman puts it, might help us offer these gestures with more care. To ask, through these gestures, "What are you going through?" To say through our touch, "I do choose."

SUFFERING AND SPIRITUALITY

There is a long history in Christianity of understanding bodily suffering as an opportunity to draw near to God. The apostle Paul speaks mysteriously of a "thorn in the flesh" from which he prayed to be delivered. But the only answer he receives to his prayer is this: "Power is made perfect in weakness." So Paul stops asking for relief and begins instead to embrace his suffering as part of his vocation: "I will boast all the more gladly of my weaknesses," he writes, "so that the power of Christ may dwell in me . . . for whenever I am weak, then I am strong" (II Corinthians 12:8–10).

Other Christians have found it fruitful to understand their suffering in this way. The twelfth-century abbess Hildegard of Bingen came to understand that her body's vulnerability to illness also made her vulnerable to the Holy Spirit. She had what medieval medicine referred to as an "airy temperament," a bodily permeability that opened her both to recurring sickness and to God. If she had enjoyed more "security of the flesh," she believed, the inspiration of the Holy Spirit would not have dwelt in her so strongly, opening her to visions of what she called "the Living Light." Two centuries later, the anchorite Julian of Norwich would pray to fall ill so that she might understand more thoroughly Christ's own suffering and be made vulnerable enough to receive visions and teachings from God.

Is there something about being healthy and well that prevents us from deepening our vision of the world, that keeps us from sensing God's presence in all of life? Perhaps there is. Perhaps suffering makes us more attentive to the miracle of this world. Simone Weil believed that only those who have known both joy and suffering could "hear the universe as the vibration of the word of God." Joy alone is not enough.

What is it we learn when our bodies are in pain? The psalmist mistrusts those who have not suffered, those who "have no pain," whose "bodies are sound and sleek" (Psalm 73:3–9). Such people are prideful and prone to violence, gossip, and folly. They believe themselves to be invulnerable. They lack the compassion that bodily suffering can teach.

I have learned how suffering can teach compassion from my sister, Diane. Soon after she was born, what at first seemed like a bad diaper rash seemed to take over her entire body. Her skin became red and hot and unbearably itchy; when she scratched it, it broke open into painful sores. As she grew, it also brought unwanted attention to her body by classmates, who teased her about her broken, weeping skin. "Allergies" caused her skin to erupt, the doctors told us, and my parents tried everything, from traditional medicine to alternative treatments, to find some relief for her.

Years and years of my sister's life passed in this way. Years and years of chronic suffering for which there seemed to be no remedy. Every doctor had a different idea to try. During the worst years, my sister was often in bed, and my parents took turns sitting up with her in the night. I remember the tender care they gave her—the waterless baths of lotion gently applied and even more gently wiped away, the cold washcloths wrapped around her burning arms and legs, the salves and ointments, the books read aloud over the long days and nights in bed.

As she got older, my sister learned which foods she should not eat; she learned to avoid, as best she could, environmental toxins. She found, through terrible trial and error, which doctors, and which medicines, could help. Then, during college, my sister announced that she would be spending her junior year in Bogota, Colombia. Oh no, I thought. How will she manage? What if she gets sick? What if she needs us, and we're not there?

She did get sick in Colombia. And she took herself to a doctor and got the help she needed, all on her own. She also took a long look at the world around her and discovered a vocation. After her time in Colombia, she arranged to go to Chile to work in a barrio-based popular education program. And then she left for El Salvador, to work for a nongovernmental human rights organization. Her job was to accompany Salvadoran human rights workers, to bear witness to their work: taking depositions from survivors of massacres, photographing bodies that turned up in fields, in forests, on the sides of the roads. She explained her commitment to this work to me like this: "I didn't want all those years in bed to be wasted."

I don't think I really understood what she meant by this until she came home from El Salvador. Life with the human rights organization had been intense. They all lived together in one house, behind a steel security door, and ventured out to do their work only in groups, never alone. My sister returned with a roll of film in her camera of a birthday party with her colleagues that she wanted to get developed. When the film came back, the birthday party pictures were there, but so were pictures of a dead man whose body bore the marks of torture, one of the victims of the Salvadoran death squads whose suffering my sister had helped to document.

I suddenly understood what my sister, my little sister who had suffered so terribly throughout her childhood, had done. She had taken her own suffering in both her hands and placed it on the altar of this world. What might have isolated her from her fellow human beings, what might have made her grow bitter and mean, had instead opened her heart so wide that she had room for the world's worst pain. How had that happened? Did her suffering create in her a desire to alleviate suffering? Did the way my parents tended her body teach her how to care for the bodies of others? Did those years in bed, in pain, sharpen her attention to what truly matters? Certainly it could have been otherwise. But somehow my sister had been given, through suffering, the courage to ask, "What are you going through?" Even when the answer was unbearable.

This is not to say that only people who have known great suffering are capable of compassion. Nor do I mean to suggest that we should seek out suffering. If I could turn back time and give my sister a childhood free of pain, I would do it in a second. What I do mean to say, though, is that when suffering comes, as it will, it might isolate us from other suffering people—or it might bring us into solidarity with them. If we have been trying to honor our bodies and the bodies of others in the midst of everyday life, if we have been attending to the sacredness of the body when we bathe and dress, eat and drink, run and rest and love, we may be better equipped to continue to honor the body when the body is in pain. And we might gain compassion, in our suffering, for the suffering of others, compassion that might change our lives.

"Touch Me and See"

A few years ago, I received a phone call at home from the nurse-practitioner whom I see for my health care. I'd had an abnormal pap smear, she said, and would need to make an appointment with a gynecological oncologist to see what was going on. As I held onto the phone, listening to her, I felt like I was on a boat that had become unmoored from the shore of my life. The voices of my husband and my daughter, talking and laughing in the kitchen, seemed to grow distant and faint. I didn't even have a diagnosis, and yet I already felt alone and afraid.

As it turned out, I did not have cancer. But I have not forgotten that feeling of loneliness and fear that engulfed me when I thought I might. The body's suffering, and even our fear of what our body might one day suffer, can create a terrible loneliness in us. The psalmist expresses this when he writes in Psalm 22, "My God, my God, why have you forsaken me?" And Jesus gives voice to this great loneliness when he cries out the words of that psalm from the cross.

Theologian John Koenig writes, "When we are very

ill, we are brought to the place where life and death meet. For Christians, this place is the cross. Yet in the central mystery of our faith, the cross is also a prelude to new life."

That bodily suffering can be both an end and a beginning is a mystery indeed. It is a mystery I cannot explain but can only contemplate with awe. I think of how my sister's suffering, which so often left her and our family feeling helpless and without hope, opened a path to her life's work. I think of the woman for whom breast cancer meant a new life of assisting refugees. I think of the residents of Interfaith House, whose ill and broken bodies are cared for and whose spirits are nurtured in a community that seeks their fullest possible healing and offers them nothing less than new life.

But I also think of the Salvadoran man whose photo my sister took to document his suffering and to resist the future suffering of others. His end was terrible, terrible, and the truth of that will never change. Where is his new beginning?

My sister cherishes the Lord's Supper, the place where the central mysteries of Christian faith are enacted. She has a profound appreciation for Jesus' suffering and loves to gather, week after week, with others who are trying to take the shape of their lives from the cross. Jesus' suffering does not give her back those years in bed. And it doesn't make the death of those who die by violence any less tragic or unbearable. But when the community gathers for communion, a space opens up that can hold both suffering and healing, endings and

Honoring the Suffering Body

beginnings, life and death and resurrection. A space opens up for hope.

I write these lines in Eastertide, one week after Easter. In this season, it is Jesus' resurrected body that teaches us that bodies matter. In the Resurrection narratives of the New Testament, Jesus insists on his body: "Look at my hands and my feet," he says in Luke's Gospel. "See that it is I myself. Touch me and see" (Luke 24:39). Offering his hands and feet for inspection, Jesus gives his followers the foundation of the new vision that will be required of them as they try to follow him when he is no longer walking and talking by their side. "Touch me," he says, "and *see.*" Jesus offers his body as the lens through which the disciples must look if they—and we—are to be able to ask our suffering neighbor, "What are you going through?" It is his body, wounded yet living, that gives us the courage to say, "I do choose."

The book of Revelation imagines a day when "death will be no more; mourning and crying and pain will be no more" (Revelation 21:4). We live in the hope of that day, but we do not yet live in that day. We can, however, bear witness to that day when we honor our bodies and the bodies of others, when we delight in our embodied selves, when we cherish and protect the bodies of those around us.

Through the vulnerability of our bodies, God has given us into the care of one another. What tender responsibility. What joy, what pain. Thanks be to God.

References

PREFACE

The quotation from Jane Kenyon is from her poem "Cages," in *From Room to Room* (Farmington, Maine: Alicejamesbooks, 1978), p. 35.

CHAPTER ONE

Kathryn Tanner's book *Theories of Culture: A New Agenda for Theology* (Minneapolis: Augsburg Fortress, 1997) was an important influence on this chapter. The quotation from St. Jerome can be found in Peter Brown, *The Body and Society* (New York: Columbia University Press, 1988), p. 317. Brown's book was another crucial influence on my thinking about the body.

CHAPTER TWO

The image of the body as an oyster trapped inside a shell is from Plato's *Phaedrus,* trans. W. C. Helmbold and W. G. Rabinowitz (New York: Bobbs-Merrill, 1956), p. 34. I have learned a great deal about how to honor the body from the poetry and prose of Mark Doty. Mark Doty's poem "Atlantis" can be found in *Atlantis* (New York: HarperCollins, 1995), pp. 55–56. Jamie Kalven and Patsy Evans tell the story of Patsy's rape and its effect on their family and their perceptions of the world in *Working with Available Light: A Family's World After Violence* (New York: Norton, 1999). The quotation from Martin Luther can be found in John H. Primus's essay in Tamara C. Eskenazi, Daniel J. Harrington, and William H. Shea, eds., *The Sabbath in Jewish and Christian Traditions* (New York: Crossroad, 1991), p. 100. An excellent discussion of early Christian understandings of the body can be found in Peter Brown's *The Body and Society.*

CHAPTER THREE

Kay Bessler Northcutt's account of her mother's last bath appears in our personal correspondence. The quotations from Diane Ackerman's *A Natural History of the Senses* (New York: Random House, 1990) are from pages 57 and 296. Elizabeth Bishop is quoted from her poem "The

Shampoo," in *The Complete Poems 1927–1979* (New York: Farrar, Straus & Giroux, 1980), p. 84. The quotation from Kathleen Norris is from *The Quotidian Mysteries: Laundry, Liturgy, and "Women's Work"* (Mahwah, N.J.: Paulist Press, 1998), pp. 40–42. Hillel is quoted from Louis Jacobs's essay "The Body in Jewish Worship," in *Religion and the Body*, ed. Sarah Coakley (Cambridge: Cambridge University Press, 1997), p. 76. The quotations from *The Rule of St. Benedict* are from chapter 53, verses 12–15 (RB 1980), ed. Timothy Fry, O.S.B. (Collegeville, Minn.: The Liturgical Press, 1981).

Chapter Four

For the discussion of piercing and tattooing in this chapter, I am indebted to Tom Beaudoin, *Virtual Faith: The Irreverent Spiritual Quest of Generation X* (San Francisco: Jossey-Bass, 1998), and Joan Jacobs Brumberg, *The Body Project: An Intimate History of American Girls* (New York: Vintage Books, 1997). Darcey Steinke is quoted from an interview conducted by Susan Gossling, posted at http://www.goucher.edu/cwpromo/kratz/Steinke_interview.htm, May 2, 2000. The quotation from Daniel Mendelsohn is from *The Elusive Embrace: Desire and the Riddle of Identity* (New York: Knopf, 1999), p. 66. The quotations from the *New York Times* are from Peter T. Kilborn's article "Prosperity Builds Mounds of Cast-Off Clothes," July 19, 1999.

CHAPTER FIVE

Laurie Colwin is quoted from pages 2–5 of her *More Home Cooking: A Writer Returns to the Kitchen* (New York: HarperCollins, 1993). The quotation from Leon R. Kass is from *The Hungry Soul: Eating and the Perfecting of Our Nature* (New York: Free Press, 1994), p. 2. Barbara Grizzuti Harrison is quoted from pages 16 and 31 of her memoir *An Accidental Autobiography* (Boston: Houghton Mifflin, 1996). The quotation from Anita Desai's novel *Fasting, Feasting* (New York: Houghton Mifflin, 2000) is from page 224. Marya Hornbacher's *Wasted: A Memoir of Anorexia and Bulimia* (New York: HarperCollins, 1998) is quoted from pages 6, 118, and 119. The quotation from Mary Douglas is from her *Purity and Danger: An Analysis of Concepts of Pollution and Taboo* (London: Routledge, 1966), p. 57. I am very much indebted to Elizabeth Ehrlich's wonderful book *Miriam's Kitchen* (New York: Penguin Books, 1997). I quote from pages 16, 24, 128, 129, and 293. Garret Keizer is quoted from pages 448 and 449 of his article "A Time to Keep Kosher," in *The Christian Century* (Apr. 19–26, 2000).

CHAPTER SIX

The Colwin quotation is from *More Home Cooking,* pp. 2 and 4. The quotation from Anne Lamott's *Traveling Mercies* (New York: Pantheon Books, 1999) is from page

197. Elias Canetti's account of the Passover seders of his childhood can be found in *The Memoirs of Elias Canetti* (New York: Farrar, Straus & Giroux, 1999), p. 25. Diana Ventura is quoted from her unpublished paper "My Journey to an Embodied Ministry!" prepared for the Field Education Practicum at the University of Chicago Divinity School. I am grateful to Diana for allowing me to quote from her work and for our ongoing conversation about religion and the body.

Chapter Seven

The quotation from Barbara Grizzuti Harrison's *An Accidental Autobiography* is from page 194. Patsy Neal, Margherita Duncan, and Steve McKinney are quoted from Diane Ackerman, *Deep Play* (New York: Vintage Books, 1999), pp. 24–25, 32, and 89. The quotation from Amy M. Hollywood is from her essay "Transcending Bodies," published in *Religious Studies Review,* Jan. 1999, 25(1), p. 13. Henry David Thoreau is quoted from pages 594–598 of his essay "Walking," published in *The Portable Thoreau,* ed. Carl Bode (New York: Penguin Books, 1977). Galway Kinnell's poem "The Tragedy of Bricks" appears in *When One Has Lived a Long Time Alone* (New York: Knopf, 1999), p. 4. The quotation from *The Rule of St. Benedict* is from chapter 48, verse 8. Lauren Artress is quoted from her book *Walking a Sacred Path: Rediscovering the Labyrinth as a Spiritual Tool* (New York: Riverhead Books, 1995), pp. 71 and 99. I am greatly indebted to Dorothy C. Bass for her work on sabbath keeping. See *Practicing Our Faith: A Way of Life for a Searching People,* ed. Dorothy C. Bass (San Francisco: Jossey-Bass, 1997); see also her book *Receiving the Day: Christian Practices for Opening the Gift of Time* (San Francisco: Jossey-Bass, 2000). She is quoted from page 79 of her essay "Keeping Sabbath," in *Practicing Our Faith.* The quotations from Abraham Joshua Heschel are from his book *The Sabbath: Its Meaning for Modern Man* (New York: Farrar, Straus & Giroux, 1951), pp. 8, 14, and 18.

CHAPTER EIGHT

Saint Augustine is quoted from his *Confessions,* trans. Rex Warner (New York: NAL/Dutton, 1963), p. 181. The quotation summarizing the poet Audre Lorde's understanding of the erotic is from James B. Nelson and Sandra P. Longfellow, *Sexuality and the Sacred: Sources for Theological Reflection* (Louisville, Ky.: Westminster/John Knox, 1994), p. 72. Mark Doty is quoted from his memoir *Heaven's Coast* (New York: HarperCollins, 1996), pp. 17 and 20, and from his memoir *Firebird* (New York: HarperCollins, 1999), p. 119. Hornbacher is quoted from *Wasted,* p. 53. Martin Amis is quoted from page 125 of his memoir *Experience* (New York: Hyperion, 2000). Luther's sermon on marriage can be found in *Luther's Works,* ed. Walther I. Brandt, Vol. 45 (Philadelphia: Muhlenberg Press, 1962), pp. 17–49. A discussion of the

United Methodist Church and United Church of Christ's sexual ethics for single people can be found in Karen Lebacqz's essay "Appropriate Vulnerability," in Nelson and Longfellow's *Sexuality and the Sacred,* pp. 256–261.

CHAPTER NINE

Virginia Woolf is quoted from her essay "On Being Ill," in *The Moment and Other Essays* (Orlando, Fla.: Harcourt Brace, 1948), p. 11. I was greatly influenced in this chapter by Elaine Scarry, *The Body in Pain: The Making and Unmaking of the World* (Oxford: Oxford University Press, 1985). The quotations from Simone Weil are from *Waiting for God,* trans. Emma Craufurd (New York: Harper-Perennial, 2001; originally published in 1951), pp. 64 and 79. The prayer attributed to Maimonides appears in Harry Friedenwald, *The Jews and Medicine* (Baltimore: Johns Hopkins Press, 1944), p. 29. The quotation from Art Bendixen is from Dan Perreten, "Healing the Homeless," *The Park Ridge Center Bulletin,* July/Aug. 1999, p. 7. Hildegard of Bingen's discussion of how her "airy temperament" makes her vulnerable not only to illness but to the inspiration of the Holy Spirit as well can be found in her *Liber divinorum operum* in the *Patrologia Latina,* ed. J.-P. Migne (Paris: Garnier, 1882), *197*(1038a). See Barbara Newman, *Sister of Wisdom: St. Hildegard's Theology of the Feminine* (Berkeley: University of California Press, 1987) for an excellent study of Hildegard.

Julian of Norwich records her desire to fall ill in her *Showings,* trans. Edmund Colledge, O.S.A. and James Walsh, S.J. (Mahwah, N.J.: Paulist Press, 1978), pp. 125–126. Koenig is quoted from his essay "Healing," in *Practicing Our Faith,* p. 151.

The Author

———

S tephanie Paulsell is a lecturer on ministry at Harvard Divinity School. She is one of the authors of *Practicing Our Faith: A Way of Life for a Searching People* and coeditor, with L. Gregory Jones, of *The Scope of Our Art: The Vocation of Theological Teachers*. She received a Ph.D. in religion and literature from the University of Chicago in 1993 and has taught at the University of Chicago Divinity School, Catholic Theological Union, and Valparaiso University. She is an ordained minister in the Christian Church (Disciples of Christ).

Index

LaVergne, TN USA
04 November 2009
163056LV00004B/119/P